Praise

CW00542160

'Amanda has a huge depth
extensive knowledge – I lo'
this new third dimension with the support tools.'
— **Steve Gurney,** Top New Zealand multisport
    athlete, nine-time winner of the Coast to
    Coast race

'Amanda moves you toward your real goal, and best
of all, she makes it an adventure.'
— **Kathrine Switzer,** Author, Emmy Award-
    winning TV commentator and global public
    speaker

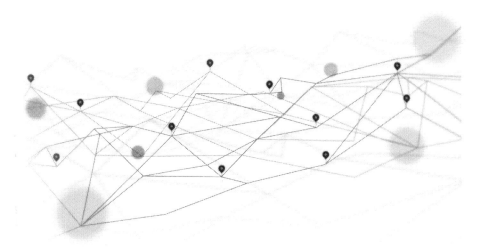

NEURAL CODING

The surprisingly
simple way to create
unthinkable change

DR AMANDA FOO-RYLAND

R^ethink

This edition first published in Great Britain in 2023
by Rethink Press (www.rethinkpress.com)

© Copyright Amanda Foo-Ryland

First published in 2011 as *This Is It!* by Amanda Mortimer

All rights reserved. No part of this publication may be
reproduced, stored in or introduced into a retrieval system, or transmitted, in any form, or by any means (elec-
tronic, mechanical, photocopying, recording or otherwise)
without the prior written permission of the publisher.

The right of Amanda Foo-Ryland to be identified as the
author of this work has been asserted by her in accordance
with the Copyright, Designs and Patents Act 1988.

This book is sold subject to the condition that it shall not,
by way of trade or otherwise, be lent, resold, hired out, or
otherwise circulated without the publisher's prior consent
in any form of binding or cover other than that in which it
is published and without a similar condition including this
condition being imposed on the subsequent purchaser.

I dedicate this book to my Uncle Peter, without whom this journey would never have started. Thanks so much for your parting gift.

Contents

Foreword

I am strong. I am relatively successful. I am a *sceptic*! Yes – wary, cautious, not easily convinced.

That is why Amanda Foo-Ryland has blown me away with this book. I arrogantly thought I was one of the least likely people to need it, so when I began to read, I soon realised that Amanda had set me down in front of a mirror and began peeling away my layers. I was shocked.

What did I see? That I am as blocked and immobile on some issues as the next person – even worse perhaps, as I've stubbornly let my scepticism prevent me from looking at different ways of moving forwards.

Have you ever wondered why it is easier to clean out your friend's garage or wardrobe and impossible to do your own? Amanda explains why: it's because we're *emotionally involved* with our own stuff.

It's the same with our lives. It's not about 'cleaning' at all. It's about our ability to let go, make space for the new, take risks and do something differently. It's about fear of loss of the old and familiar even if it is useless, and equal fear of the new and unknown. We block ourselves on purpose, but we can't help it.

My strong old sceptic mantra for change was, 'Just take action'. However, day after busy day, I, like you, am assaulted with endless reasons – real, valid and compelling, like deadlines or family time-constraints – to postpone doing what I really need or really *want* to do. I get heaps of 'small stuff' done, and it often is marginally significant. However, most of the time it's not the *real* thing. I let small stuff logjam me. Every time I do that, I kick myself for another wasted opportunity.

A few years ago, an experienced author friend of mine asked how I was progressing with my latest book. When I said I just hadn't had time to write lately, he quietly said, 'There will always be a million things that will prevent you from just sitting down and writing.' I felt ashamed of myself.

When I can break the logjam and get to the important things, I rejoice in the sense of accomplishment.

My problem, and yours too, I suspect, is that it seems so hard.

Amanda Foo-Ryland shows us how to move forwards. More shockingly, she makes it simple and, more embarrassingly, she makes it fun. She is the only person I know who says, 'Fantastic,' when you say your life is a disastrous 2 on a scale of 1 to 10. 'It gives us more to work with,' she quips.

For too long we've been led to believe that our procrastinating denial of dreams or constant sabotage of our own success is a neurosis worthy of psychiatric analysis. Amanda can show you how to stretch a string across the ground and give you a visual example of how to change your life. Now, this is the kind of therapy I like!

Amanda doesn't hold back on herself, either. It's always reassuring to see that the expert can also fall off her bike. Amanda not only shows you how to get back on it; she'll show you how to grow from the experience. Her wisdom and honed technique come from both her own experience and her conscientious work with hundreds of clients. She definitely moves you towards your real goal, and best of all, she makes it an adventure.

Go for it!

Kathrine Switzer, Author, Emmy Award-winning TV commentator and global public speaker

Kathrine is also best known as the woman who challenged the all-male rule of the famous Boston Marathon by being the first woman to officially register and run the race, creating an international uproar. She went on to run thirty-seven marathons, won the New York City Marathon, and led the drive to get the women's marathon into the Olympic Games by organising 400 women's races in twenty-seven countries for a million women. Her books include *Marathon Woman, Running and Walking for Women Over 40* and *26.2 Marathon Stories* (co-authored with Roger Robinson). Kathrine lives in both New Zealand and the United States of America. She runs daily and competes often.

Introduction

What's it all about?

How serious are you about living the life you want? Are you ready to make changes that could transform the way you feel every single day? This book is designed to create serious, unconscious change using Neural Coding, your unconscious mind and a new interactive experience.

It is like having your own Neural Coder right there with you, taking you through the processes with our easy to use Virtual Coaching platform.

You might be thinking, what is Neural Coding? It is a blend of Neuro-Linguistic Programming, Timeline Therapy and Hypnosis, essentially an NLP upgrade.

It works a little like this. Imagine you have an app on your phone that is not working – you delete it, right? Then you install one that does the job for you. Neural Coding is just like this: we find the problem, delete it and install a solution in its place. We are looking for glitchy programmes running in your neurology, deleting them and installing a new solution.

It's fast and it lasts.

Interested? Then I have some more questions for you. . .

Have you ever wanted to change things in your life, but no matter how much will and determination you've got, you haven't been able to do it? You're absolutely resolute, yet two weeks later that same old behaviour comes back. Have you ever, full of conviction, said to yourself, 'I'm going to start a fitness regime.' And you've done it. You've bought your gym membership and started going. You've made a conscious decision to get fit. You really want to, however, three months later, it's been a waste of money. You didn't keep going, and you're still the same size, weight and level of fitness that you were when you started – or worse. Perhaps you made a conscious decision to stop smoking, or to stop eating so much unhealthy food, but there you were puffing away and stuffing your face just a short time later.

Most of my clients come to me having already tried many times to change their lives and eliminate destructive behaviours. If these habits could really be broken consciously, nobody would need to come to me at all. They would just decide, 'Right, I'm going to change,' and then go ahead and do it. If only it were that easy.

The problem is that automatic functions are controlled by our *unconscious* mind (also referred to as the sub-conscious). Those bad habits we've developed, those automatic self-defeating behaviours, are not regulated by conscious thoughts and willpower at all. Yet, most of our attempts to change are based on conscious methods. We make a decision, create clear goals, decide how we're going to get from A to B, use affirmations and monitor our progress until we get where we want to be. These conscious methods are useful up to a point, but any change they bring about is often temporary. Before long, the same old habits return and we find ourselves back where we started, but more frustrated than ever.

Now I'd like you to play along with me for a moment. Put the book down, and fold your arms in front of you. OK. That should have been pretty easy. Now, fold your arms the other way. Change which arm is in front. That was probably more difficult, so you had to actually think about what you were doing. You had to bring the instruction into your conscious mind and work out what to do. What this tells us is that how you cross your arms is normally a completely unconscious, automatic behaviour. There are lots of behaviours which we do automatically. The question is, which automatic behaviours are not helpful? Which ones do you want to change? In order for them to change, that change has to happen at the unconscious level.

If you haven't already, you can unfold your arms now. Hopefully that's given you some food for thought and makes it clear that what we need is something that works alongside those useful, conscious techniques, but which also speaks to our unconscious mind.

And that's just what you'll discover in this book.

I'd like you to take a moment to think about your book collection. Have you bought books in the past, hoping they would help move your life forwards? Perhaps special diet books, life coaching, popular psychology, philosophical or lifestyle books? Which of them jump out at you as the ones that really made a difference? What springs to mind if you're asked, 'Which books have changed your life?' I'm guessing there are only one or two. We buy these books (and even get around to reading some of them), but a large number of them end up back on the bookshelf, virtually forgotten about.

Sitting on a shelf gathering dust is not the place for this book.

We will, of course, make use of some of the conscious life coaching tools that you may have come across before, because we need to engage the conscious mind in what we're going to do. The key difference is that we'll also work directly with your unconscious mind, so that they start working in harmony and supporting each other.

If you work with me, we can connect with the truly amazing resources you already have within you. The unconscious mind we keep referring to is awe-inspiring in its infinite intelligence. Did you know it can process approximately eleven million things every second?[1] Now that's powerful. Compare it to the mere five to seven things that the conscious mind can handle at one time.[2] Some readers might be tempted to suggest that the number of tasks the conscious mind can deal with simultaneously is largely determined by gender, but I couldn't possibly comment!

The science of Neural Coding will be at the foundation of how we access the massive power of your unconscious mind. It really is a science. The originators were professors. One, Richard Bandler, was a professor of mathematics. The other, John Grinder, a professor of linguistics. Both also had degrees in psychology. They built on the work produced by previous giants of psychology and hypnosis, such as Milton Erickson, Virginia Satir and Carl Rogers, to understand and harness the language of the unconscious. What they

---

1   K Abbasi, 'A riot of divergent thinking', *Journal of the Royal Society of Medicine*, Oct (2011), 104(10) 391, www.ncbi.nlm.nih.gov/pmc/articles/PMC3184540/#:~:text=Divergent%20thinking%20is%20the%20ability,different%20answers%20to%20a%, accessed 20 June 2023
2   K Abbasi, 'A riot of divergent thinking'

created was hugely powerful, and quick to deliver long lasting results.

There are plenty of books on Neuro-Linguistic Programming, and many of them are excellent. However, they can be heavy going and loaded down with theories and explanations. One of my aims in this book is to make change easy as we have upgraded from NLP to Neural Coding, which is fast, simple and does what it says on the tin. You re-code yourself.

More than just a book

We all have different ways that we learn best; some of us need to see things to know what to do. Some need to listen and some to read. Therefore, we've created a system that has something for everyone; you could call it a 3D book. Every process described in the book is recorded for you, so that you can let me walk you through each one personally. We've created a whole support system, designed to give you every possible chance to succeed. You can access your personal, virtual coach at our website:

https://tinyurl.com/neuralcoding

This link will give you special access to a section with all the resources available to you.

So, just by purchasing this book, you've bought *me* as your virtual coach, right there at your fingertips.

When you've explored all the resources that are there for you, I really think you'll agree that we've got a unique and exciting concept in Your Life Live It.

I'm so passionate about the tools we're sharing in this book, and so confident that they can make a huge difference to people's lives, that I want as many people as possible to discover them, understand them and use them. Everyone deserves the chance to change their lives for the better. Therefore, no matter how busy you are, and whatever your financial situation or opportunity to attend courses, it is all here for you, at a time that suits you. No journeys to make, no bad hotel coffee and uncomfortable chairs to sit on all day, no planning who's going to watch the kids and figuring out how you can afford the fees. It's all here, in your own home. All I ask is that you come to this book with a genuine desire to change, and that you're prepared to put some effort into creating the life you dream of.

Why am I reading this book, anyway?

If you've bought this book, there's something about your life you want to change. Really, there is! You would have picked something quite different if this wasn't the case. You may not know it yet, but you've already started your journey. As you read these words, your conscious and unconscious minds are already wondering just how easy it will be to change with all these tools. I don't know what it is that you want to change: perhaps just one small aspect of your life isn't quite as you'd like it, or maybe the whole thing needs a revamp. Either way, you want to reach out for a brighter, more inspiring future. Together, that's just what we can do. Not because I have some kind of magic wand up my sleeve, and not if you expect changes just to happen, with no effort on your part. This book is for people who really want to create a better, more vibrant and wonderful future for themselves, and are ready to do what it takes to get there.

Through this book I'll be putting some really powerful tools into your hands. It's all here, waiting for you to take action. Every day that you're alive the choices you make contribute to the sum total of your life. It's up to you to really live this day, making powerful, dynamic choices. Or you could let it drift through your fingers almost unnoticed, much the same as yesterday and the day before.

Hence the title of this book: *Neural Coding*. I can show you the way, but only you can decide to really live it – or not.

ONE
Who Do I Think I Am?

Why should I be able to help you change things you may have been struggling with for years? How am I qualified to guide you on this fantastic journey you're about to embark on?

At this point, many personal development books would launch into the 'desperate loser-turned-winner' stories; the tales of transformation from morbid obesity to slim, trim and fit; from the depths of poverty to the heights of wealth and comfort; from shy misfit to confident, relaxed and socially at ease.

Don't get me wrong. Those stories have their place, and I've got my fair share of them. Some will certainly pop up at relevant points throughout the book. What I'm trying to say is, I'm not a 'Look at the perfect life

I have – you can have one too!' kind of coach. Yes, I've been overweight, a smoker, divorced, unemployed, cheated on. . . lots of the stuff that happens to so many of us and makes us think, 'This is *not* how I want life to be!' Those experiences might have given me a personal insight into your problems, and may help you to feel that I really do understand where you're coming from. However, they don't in themselves mean much – other than illustrating that I'm a normal person who has experienced lots of the ups and downs in life that so many people have. What *really* makes me think I can help you on your journey is the fact that I've done it before. Many, many times. While I may have changed my own life in significant ways, what really counts is that I've helped many *other* people to change *their* lives; all of them different, with their own unique personalities, problems and desires. I've watched the tools and techniques you'll find in this book transform people. I've guided them and walked with them as they've made *real, lasting* changes, and I'm totally in awe of the capacity of people to transform themselves and their lives when they have the right tools.

Now you might already be itching to get on with your journey and to start taking control of your future. If that's the case, great! I certainly don't want to stand in your way. Feel free to jump ahead, where you'll start discovering how to speak in the language of your unconscious mind, how to harness its power, and you'll get the chance to test out some simple, effective exercises that I hope will whet your appetite to delve deeper. If you do jump ahead, you can always come back later to visit me here if your curiosity gets the better of you!

On the other hand, if you'd like to know a little more about this woman who is promising that you *can* change your life, even if you've already tried and failed before, possibly many times, then read on. After all, why should you simply believe me when I hold out my hand to you and say, 'Trust me – I know how to get where you want to go'?

I run a successful coaching company that straddles the globe. I have spent hundreds of hours dealing with clients from all walks of life and with all sorts of different goals in the areas of health, sport, business and personal life. How did I get here? What qualifies me to write a book like this?

I certainly haven't had anything like a 'perfect' life, however, one thing I *have* had is a constant fascination with human potential and development. It really all began when I was just eighteen and started working for the Estée Lauder Corporation, the cosmetic industry giant. After my first week with them, I met the glamorous woman who was going to train me to be a beauty advisor. I watched her at work, and quickly realised that I wanted to do her job. When I asked her about it over lunch, she raised her beautifully shaped eyebrows and delicately made it clear that I had a long way to go and a lot to learn before I could even begin to think about becoming a training executive like her. There were 1,200 Estée Lauder beauty advisors in the UK, most of whom had ambitions of becoming a training executive, and there were only twelve training executive positions in the whole country. She outlined all the steps I would have to go through before the corporation would even consider me – and I hadn't even completed my basic training yet.

It didn't put me off. I knew I wanted to do it, so I got my head down, worked really hard and did everything she had outlined. I was actually using some Neural Coding techniques then that I'll share with you later – I just didn't know it at the time. After less than two years working on the counter, I went for an interview for the job of 'field training executive'. The interview was a daunting prospect and would take place in 'the Big City' – London. It was meant to be a practice run; a bit of experience in preparation for future 'real' interviews and yet, for whatever reason, at the tender age of twenty, I felt confident as I made the long journey to Head Office. Maybe it was the bright red power suit that did it. The smart, high-heeled shoes I could barely walk in certainly made me feel very much the young executive! Perhaps it was the lovely London cabbie who drove me to my interview and believed me when I said I was going to get the job. Whatever it was, I surprised everyone (except, perhaps, myself) by landing that job and becoming their youngest ever field training executive.

The reality of what I now had to do soon hit home. I had a shaky start, which you'll hear about later in the book. However, as I settled into the job, I quickly realised that this was exactly the right place for me. I steadily worked my way up, becoming the Regional Training Manager for the North of England, Scotland and Ireland, then Regional Education Manager for Europe, Middle East and Africa for Clinique. By the time I left the corporation in 2000, I had spent fourteen of my sixteen years with them immersed in human development.

I left to work with my then-partner (now my husband) in his advertising agency in Leeds, Yorkshire, running the training for all 120 staff. I still got a huge buzz from my work, yet I was beginning to feel there was something missing. I was becoming more and more fascinated by the field of personal development. I was trying to figure out how I could continue my work, but in a way that focused on helping people achieve their *personal* goals. Of course, it was rewarding to help people develop within a corporate setting – watching a young eighteen-year-old learn to run their own counter and manage five staff, or being promoted out of their store to become an Account Executive – but I realised I wanted to do something on a much more personal level.

At about this time, Uncle Peter passed away suddenly. I felt really bad that I hadn't been able to attend his funeral, so when I visited my aunt shortly afterwards,

I asked if there was anything I could do to help. She explained that Uncle Peter's company would soon run out of patience waiting for the return of their paperwork, but she had been dreading clearing out his office. She couldn't face coming across all the little personal things that she was bound to find there, so would I please clear the office for her?

I spent a whole day going through his office, and it was as difficult as I'd expected. Everything I found that reminded me of Uncle Peter also reminded me that he was gone. I quite deliberately left his briefcase to last, as I knew it was most likely to have the deeply personal things that Auntie Rosemary had been dreading finding. I needed a bit of time to prepare myself for whatever I might find there.

And then something really quite special happened. It seemed like a wonderful, parting gift from Uncle Peter. When I opened his briefcase, I found paperwork that indicated Uncle Peter had signed up for a certification course in life coaching. I looked at all the information about the course and it sounded both fascinating and inspiring. I felt a rush of excitement. The course hadn't actually started yet, so I phoned Newcastle College, explained the circumstances and asked if it would be possible for me to take Uncle Peter's place on the course. After some discussion, they agreed.

So, thanks to Uncle Peter, I trained and qualified as a life coach. It took me three years of studying around a full-time job to get my full certification and diploma. I was then able to set up my own business called 'Sales Training Portugal'. I was able to use my corporate training experience to work with businesses in Portugal (where we now lived) and I was also able to offer life coaching to individuals. I was definitely getting closer to what I really wanted to do. I was still helping businesses to make more money, but I was also helping individual clients get more out of their own lives.

It still felt like there was something missing, though.

For example, a client might come to me saying, 'What's wrong with me? I keep repeating this same, destructive behaviour and I don't know why. It's not like I *want* to be like this. I just can't stop it! What can I do?'

The life coaching skills I'd learned couldn't really help in any lasting way. Life coaching was great, but it was all conscious. It was all about taking the client from A to B with regular follow-ups, but there we were talking about unconscious behaviour and ways of thinking that had become totally ingrained habits. Clients had already tried all sorts of things to consciously attempt to change. Some of them had already seen other life coaches to try to resolve whatever their issue was, yet six months later the old behaviours were back.

I became really curious about how it might be possible to change this kind of behaviour quickly and, more importantly, permanently. How can you help someone who believes at their core that they're just not worth it? My life coaching tool set just couldn't answer that.

I had started to read some books on NLP, thanks to my good friend Gillian Rosen. While on holiday together, lounging around the pool, she threw an NLP book at me and said, 'You should read this. It's fascinating stuff. . .'

I was pretty sceptical. I mean, 'neuro-linguistic pro-gramming' – I could hardly pronounce it, let alone understand what it meant! Who came up with that snappy name, anyway? But I dipped into it, tried a couple of the simpler techniques, and realised that it really was amazingly effective. The more I read about NLP and hypnotherapy (they really do go hand in hand), the more interested I became. Before long, I was taking a practitioner level training programme in London and came out with certification in NLP, Hypnosis and Timeline Therapy®.

It completely changed the way I worked with clients, and the results were astounding. The first client I used my new skills with worked at the BBC and was ter-rified of public speaking. This was more than a little inconvenient, as he regularly had to present to groups of forty or more people.

For about forty-eight hours before any public speaking engagement he would become anxious, unable to sleep, and would sweat profusely (so much so that he actually had Botox injections under his arms to try to control it). His coping strategy was simply to put up with the symptoms.

He came to see me because his job had recently changed. He was now going to have to speak at the BAFTA awards ceremony in front of at least 200 people and several television cameras. As if that wasn't enough, in the audience would be Anne – yes, *that* Anne – the Princess Royal herself! He simply couldn't continue as he was.

With the skills I was now able to employ, that client walked out of our session with a new confidence and a belief that not only was he good at public speaking, but that he actually enjoyed it. I caught up with him some months later, after the Big Day. On the back of the speech that he'd so dreaded making, he had been invited to twelve independent presentations as the keynote speaker, and he had enjoyed every minute of each and every one of them. All of his old anxieties had completely disappeared.

What we had done in a short period of time was change his core belief (that he really wasn't a very good speaker) at an *unconscious* level. This was the kind of dramatic result that made me realise just how incredibly powerful working with the unconscious mind really was.

I wanted to learn everything I could to become the best possible coach. I read everything I could lay my hands on, applied the techniques more and more (both with myself and with my clients) and became increasingly better at helping people with their difficulties. I just couldn't get enough of it. I did my Master Practitioner training in Auckland, New Zealand, with Dr Richard Bolstad. I developed my new business, Your Life Live It in 2008. I continued to read, went back to help on the courses I'd already done, and became an instructor of Neural Coding.

I also learned new and different therapies and modalities, some of which I'll be sharing with you later in the book, but Neural Coding has remained at the core of what I do. I'm now an accredited trainer of Neural Coding, I have a degree in clinical hypnotherapy and I'm currently studying for my master's degree in clinical hypnotherapy, after which I plan to do my doctorate.

I've not told you all this to say, 'Hey, look at me, aren't I amazing?' I simply want to show you how I am constantly committed to learning, deepening my own knowledge and understanding, getting the best training I possibly can and keeping absolutely up to date with latest developments and breakthroughs. That way, I can offer people the best tools and techniques for improving their lives. The reason I want you to know this is so that when I say, 'Come with me, I really can help,' you can feel confident that it's true.

Ready, steady, GO!

As you make your way through the book, keep an eye out for the references to the website and additional resources that are available to you. I want to ensure you get the best out of your time, so I am going to be your Virtual Coder. Look out for the icons below. They're marked with these images in the margin so you can spot them easily.

This icon is for general resources, PDFs to print out and videos.

This one means I've recorded an audio clip for you to listen to.

Be ready for those moments where you recognise yourself in the stories and situations we explore and you think, 'Yes. That's me! This is what I need to deal with.'

Certain exercises and resources will resonate with you and will jump out as ones that appeal or that you know you need to act on. When that happens, promise me you'll take action. Otherwise, this book will be relegated to just another of those gathering dust on your shelf: the ones that offered hope and that seemed to have potential, but that you didn't act upon. What a waste that would be.

Instead, I hope you're ready to come with me. To start on the incredible journey that is the rest of your life. To explore everything that this unique combination of book, audio, video and website has to offer. To use the tools and techniques we'll be exploring, to learn how your mind really works, and to transform how you feel about your life every single day.

If you are, then together we can achieve exactly what we both want: you, to create the kind of life you really desire by making the changes that have eluded you for so long; and me, to know I helped you get there!

TWO

Speaking The Language Of Your Mind

I've already mentioned a few times about learning to speak in the mind's language. You may well be thinking, 'Surely my mind speaks the same language as the rest of me?'

Well, yes – and no. Obviously, you don't think in a foreign language! But if you want to consciously communicate with, and direct the power of, your unconscious, you need to become aware of how you habitually think.

Let's take a moment to demonstrate how powerful our thoughts can be (and *why* it's so important to take control of your thinking). I like to do this exercise with new clients. You can do it just by reading through the exercise here. Better still, if you have access to the

Internet, whenever you see this icon, why not head over to the website, where I've recorded a video to help you achieve a more intense experience.

Lemons to You (video)
https://tinyurl.com/neuralcoding

Enjoy!

EXERCISE: Lemons to you

I'm fortunate enough to spend three or four months of every year in beautiful Portugal. As you'd expect, we get plenty of wonderful sunny days, and I like to take my road bike out early in the mornings and cycle through the lovely countryside before the temperatures climb too high. This often takes me through the lemon groves, where at the right time of year, the aroma from all those lemons ripening on the trees is just amazing. In this exercise, we're going to be imagining one of those lemons.

So, wherever you happen to be, I want you to imagine that you've got a perfect lemon right there in front of you. Picture it there: the perfect colour, the perfect shape. You know that it's the perfect lemon. Enjoy knowing that this is your perfect lemon, with its perfectly formed skin, plump with juice and reminiscent of the sun-soaked groves it grew in.

Imagine taking a knife and cleanly cutting that perfect lemon in half, recognising that distinctive swishing sound of the knife slicing through the stiff peel and the soft, juice-filled centre of the fruit. The lemon fragrance and the juices are instantly released to float up into the air in a cloud of lemon aroma. You can almost see all those tiny particles of lemon juice and lemon oil as they fill the air. Imagine what that smells like, and what it might taste like if a little of that lemony cloud just happens to touch your tongue.

Look at the cut lemon halves and notice how some of the segments have been broken open. One of the segments is still absolutely full of rich lemon juice. Now, I'd like you to cut off a slice of that lemon. A mouth-sized slice, the kind you might pop in a cool drink. Look at that slice closely, noticing all the little sacks and segments bursting with juice just waiting to be released. Imagine you're going to pop that slice of lemon into your mouth, biting down and releasing all that juice over your tongue.

Well done, and thanks for playing along with me. Now I'd like you to take a moment to check around the inside of your mouth with your tongue. You'll almost certainly notice that there's extra saliva. I know that even sitting here writing this passage, my own mouth is watering in response to the image created in my mind. Why should that be? We know there's no lemon. I don't have a lemon in front of me and yet my mouth is reacting as though there was. I'm guessing that yours is, too. All you had was your imagination. You imagined what it looked like; you imagined what it smelled like; you imagined what it tasted like. The interesting thing is that to your body, that lemon was real. To your body, that lemon slice was about to come into your mouth, and your mouth prepared for it with extra saliva just as it would have for the real thing.

There are two things to take from this exercise. The first is the realisation that your thoughts, be they good, bad or neutral, really do have a direct impact on your body. The second is that your unconscious mind (and, as a result, the automatic processes within your body) can't tell the difference between a real experience and a vividly imagined one – they react to both just the same. There was no lemon, we both know consciously that it did not exist, and yet your unconscious mind took the image, smell and taste you created literally, producing extra saliva to cut through the acidity of something you simply imagined.

Our mind can have unwitting power over our automatic functions simply because of what and how we think. It's time to take control. In fact, this is pretty much what makes one person different from another. We're all fundamentally the same, aren't we? Human beings, made to the same basic design. The only real difference is the way we think, and for most people, that's largely automatic.

Two people can have exactly the same experience, yet view it completely differently. Even something as objectively traumatic as losing a limb in an accident can have a different impact on the people involved. One person could, understandably, see it as a total disaster and struggle to deal with the loss of the limb, while the other, equally legitimately, embraces life with renewed vigour, feeling fortunate that they survived the accident at all and determined to make sure that their life from now on will be significant and meaningful.

The only real difference between these two people is how they think about the experience. It's not that one way of thinking is right and the other wrong, simply that one way is more empowering and enabling than the other.

Most people don't take control of their thought processes at all. What's worse, left to our own devices, the vast majority of our thoughts are negative ones. Did you know that the average person has about 6,200 thoughts every day? And it's been calculated that about 80% of those are negative.[3] That's something like 5,000 negative, critical, pessimistic and miserable thoughts, however fleeting many of them might be, every day! No wonder many of us struggle to reach our true potential or live the life we want.

I'm not suggesting you'll solve all your problems by forcing yourself to take a rosy, Pollyanna approach to life. Trying to consciously view life more positively does allow people to think differently, and positive

---

3   C Johnson, 'Stuck on negative thinking' (Care Counseling, 2023), https://care-clinics.com/stuck-on-negative-thinking, accessed 12 June 2023

affirmations have their place, but telling yourself ten nice things before you leave the house each morning won't, on its own, transform your life. (And that's assuming you can keep those affirmations going for more than about a week. In my experience, that's the longest most people manage to keep at it.)

However, learning to change how you think when those negative thoughts are blocking you from reaching your goals is one of the key things we'll be looking at later in the book, and it's a fundamental part of taking control of your life.

Positives please

The next step in understanding how your mind interprets your thoughts is to explore what happens when we think in negatives. We're conditioned by society and our environment to think this way. Don't run in the corridor; No diving in the pool; Photography is not permitted; No smoking; Don't drink and drive; No tipping; Don't slip. We see and hear negatives everywhere.

But what happens in our minds when we think in negatives? Let's take a look, shall we?

Just as in the exercise above, you might find it more fun or effective to go to the website and watch the version of this exercise that I've recorded for you.

Look for the 'Blue Trees' video, then come back and join us in the book when you're done. Otherwise, simply read on.

Blue Trees (video)
https://tinyurl.com/neuralcoding

EXERCISE: The power of negatives

This is a really simple exercise, but it's important to concentrate and focus on getting it right – that's why closing your eyes and using the recorded version might make it easier for you. Be as accurate as you can.

The most important thing during this exercise is that you don't think about a blue tree. You have to try really hard not to think about just how blue that tree might be, or how yellow the canary is that's sitting at the top of the blue tree. You definitely shouldn't think about how big the canary is compared to the small blue tree it's sitting in, or about the big sign around its neck that says in bold letters, 'Changing is so easy'. Don't think about any of that.

And don't think about the fact that the canary is swaying from side to side in this blue tree and singing cheerfully to you.

What does this exercise demonstrate? It shows us how the unconscious mind can't process negatives. I'm guessing that although it was made clear all the way through the exercise that you should *not* think about the things mentioned, you ended up with an image of a blue tree with a yellow canary in it, even if it was only briefly or vaguely. Most people end up with a pretty clear image of what it was they were not meant to be thinking about. You see, our minds have to first picture the thing we're not meant to think about so we can then try to stop thinking about it!

Most of us spend a huge amount of our time focusing on what we *don't* want rather than on what we do want. For example, 'I don't want to smoke.' The problem is, the mind doesn't process the 'don't' in this thought. It simply sees, 'I want to smoke.' The thought of stopping smoking is urging you to smoke, and makes you unconsciously see yourself as a smoker.

What this means is that it's really important when we want to change something about our lives or our behaviour, that we phrase our thoughts about it in the positive. When my clients first come to see me, the vast majority of them (about 84% so far) will tell me what they *don't* want or what they want to stop doing or have less of rather than what they *do* want. Thinking like this just keeps our minds focused on what we're trying to move away from, no matter what we think we're aiming for.

So, forget any prejudices or preconceived notions you might have about 'positive thinking'. It's not just a way of trying to make the world a nicer place. It's not all sweetness and light. It's a crucial tool for getting what you want out of life. Telling children to walk in the corridors isn't a soft option in comparison to 'don't run'. It's simply more likely to help them to conform – it plants the image in their minds of orderly lines of pupils walking through the school. In contrast, 'don't run' immediately brings to mind an image of pupils rampaging through the corridors, and it's only conscious self-discipline that makes (most of) them resist. If you want to see this in action, you can watch the 'Negative suggestion' video clip on the Chapter 2 section of the website.

Then check out a world record-holding expert on the high wire, who has never fallen off. You'll see what happens to the most positive of thinkers when the negative suggestion, 'Don't fall off, don't wobble,' is planted in his head.

When you begin to think about what you want and what your goals might be, phrase them in the positive. For example, 'I don't want to be fat,' could become, 'I want to use food to help me feel slim, healthy and full of energy.'

Why not practise? Try turning these negative statements below into constructive ones that would give your unconscious mind something positive to aim for.

Negative statement	Positive statement
'I don't want to work too hard.'	'I want to have more free time to relax and have fun.'
'I want to stop smoking.'	'I want to breathe easier, be healthier and live to enjoy my life.'
'I don't want to run around after everyone else all the time.'	
'I don't want to feel so lonely and isolated.'	

Harnessing the power of the unconscious

We've now seen how our thoughts can affect us physically, and we've seen how our mind can only process positives. Now it's time to apply both of these in a simple, fun exercise that demonstrates how, if we think in the language of the mind, we can effortlessly use our unconscious to enhance performance and take us where we want to go.

As with the previous exercises, there is a recorded version of this exercise on the web for you. This is definitely one that is easier and more effective if you listen to it and actually do it. If you can't do that right now and are impatient to try it, just read the exercise through. It would be best to go to the website as soon as you can, though, to complete the experience.

How Far Can You Go? (video)
https://tinyurl.com/neuralcoding

EXERCISE: How far can you go?

Stand with your feet hip width apart. Make sure that you're standing in enough space that you can extend your arm in front of you and turn round in all directions without knocking anything over or risking an assault charge if there's anyone else in the room! Throughout this exercise, keep your feet firmly planted on the floor. They shouldn't move or change position at all.

Extend your right arm straight out in front of you, pointing straight ahead of you with your right hand. You should be looking along your arm, and should see your outstretched finger pointing away from you.

In a moment, you're going to turn your torso clockwise, to your right, keeping your feet firmly where they are, so you are twisting from the waist and hips, but keeping your feet still. You'll turn, still pointing, until you feel tightness. As soon as you feel tightness, stop and look at where your finger is pointing. Make a mental picture of where you're pointing, and then come back to centre. OK, now that you know what to do, go ahead and turn.

Once you've turned and noted where you were pointing when you felt tightness, stay standing on the same spot and relax a little. Close your eyes and imagine you are holding your hand up in front of you again, pointing straight ahead. You know exactly what it looks like, because you've just been doing it, so just picture it clearly. However, on this occasion, you notice that your hand feels light and floaty. You get a sense that your whole arm is light and floaty too, almost as though your arm and hand are suspended in mid-air on their own. It's just so effortless to keep them up there.

Imagine, now, that you start moving that arm round to the right. . . It's almost like it's moving all by itself, really easily, very light, very fluid. Your body just seems to be in flow, everything is totally relaxed and easy, so easy that you comfortably go past the original spot you were pointing at last time. In fact, you go past so easily that now you're pointing about 20 cm further than last time. Make a picture in your mind of where you would be pointing if you went 20 cm past the spot you stopped at last time. You might not know specifically, but get a sense of what you would be pointing at. Roughly where would it be if you turned about 20 cm further than the last time? Make a picture of that in your mind and notice just how light and effortless this is, how easy and in flow the body is. What would you say to yourself, what would your internal dialogue be, as you realised that you could go so easily past that original point and noticed that your hand and arm felt even lighter?

Now you notice that you've moved even further, another 5 cm more, so you've now come 25 cm further than you did originally, and you've done it with such ease. . . It feels like you could almost go all the way round, this is so light and effortless. What would it feel like to be this supple? Make a picture of where you would be pointing now that you've come 25 cm further than the original spot you pointed at. Notice again that the body is just completely fluid. Imagine what you might say to yourself now. It might reflect surprise: 'Wow, this is so easy!' And, of course, all of this is in your imagination.

Now, open your eyes. Raise that right hand for real this time and notice what happens as you start to effortlessly and easily turn and where your hand takes you.

When we do this exercise on our courses, we get at least 95% of people going much further than the extra 25 cm they imagined. I'm guessing that you certainly went further the second time than you did the first time, especially if you used a recording to help you through the exercise.

What's happening is that you're communicating in the brain's language. You've created a picture of where you want to be pointing. You've thought about how you want your body to feel – loose and fluid and light. You've tuned in to words like *lightweight, effortless, ease, flexible, fluid* – easy, positive words that allowed you to turn almost without thinking about it. Also, you thought about what your internal dialogue would be.

Of course, the first time you did the pointing exercise, I asked you to look for tightness, and that's what your brain looked for. The moment it found any feeling of tightness, you stopped.

But then we became specific about those three key things: what you would see, what you would feel and what you would hear. You communicated to your unconscious mind exactly where you wanted to go and it responded accordingly. Our unconscious mind is programmed to support what it *thinks* our aims are. It's up to us to make sure we communicate with it in a way it will understand and interpret correctly.

Unfortunately, a lot of people live their lives looking for 'tightness' – looking for the reasons why they can't do something. The unconscious will obligingly agree. When we set our mind to something we want to achieve, it's really important that we think the right way and use the right kind of language in our thoughts. If we are clear about what we will see, what we will feel, and what we will hear (internally and externally) when we have achieved what we want, then all the incredible, under-used power of our unconscious mind will support us in our efforts.

So, we've seen how our thoughts can affect us physically, and we've seen how our mind can only process positives. In the next chapter, you'll learn to make use of both of these facts in a simple, fun exercise that demonstrates how, if we think in the language of the mind, we can effortlessly use our unconscious to enhance performance and take us where we want to go.

THREE

Getting Down To Business

So, we've explored some of the ways we can engage and communicate with the unconscious mind. We need to do this so that it works in harmony with our aims rather than unwittingly hijacking them. I know the exercises we did in the last chapter gave you a taste of how effective these techniques can be. Now it's time to get down to the business of making them work for you in the areas of your life that really matter. We'll still find time to have some fun along the way, but we're about to start that exciting, scary journey towards the life you really want.

How do you score?

I need you to think carefully about your life right now: all areas of it. Health and fitness, family life, intimate relationships, finances, career, spiritual life, social life, intellectual stimulation – you name it.

Think about the whole thing. Where are you currently on a scale of one to ten, with ten being, 'I absolutely, totally and completely love this aspect of my life'?

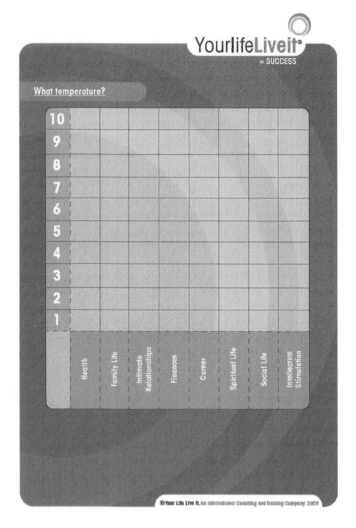

Download the 'What Temperature' PDF of the chart above to score each area of your life by ticking where you are on the scale. Alternatively, use a notebook to record your score out of ten.

What Temperature (PDF)
https://tinyurl.com/neuralcoding

Have fun with it; just go with your gut feeling when you think about that area of your life. Think of it like a holiday temperature chart. How 'hot' is each part of your life?

It's a simple enough chart, but gives valuable feedback. One glance at it should quickly show you the areas of your life that need some attention.

I don't think you're about to tell me your life's a perfect ten. If it is, that's fantastic! Even if your life is great, there's almost certainly some aspect that you'd like to make even better. If you've scored lots of 'ones', then that's even better, because you're really going to love the transformation we're heading for.

It might be a bit scary to think about shifting things that have been stuck for so long – but what a fantastic future to look forward to!

Now you need to think about what would have to change for these aspects of your life to score a ten. Don't let yourself off the hook by generalising that everything needs to change because your life's so awful. It might sound harsh, but lazy thinking like that won't help you to change a thing. In fact, it's a safe way of staying exactly where you are. Take a little time and think about it carefully. Which aspects of your life aren't exactly as you would like? What is it that's not working? What would you change if you could? Everyone's got something that they would like to feel differently about.

Now, do me a favour. Take a few minutes to think about the lowest 'temperatures' on your chart. What makes you feel so 'cold' about those parts of your life? Download the 'Hot or Cold' PDF from the website or use your notebook to write down what things need to change, and *how* they need to change in order for you to score ten out of ten for that aspect of your life. Really express why you feel the way you do about those different parts of your life right now. Have a good old rant.

Hot or Cold (PDF)
https://tinyurl.com/neuralcoding

My guess is that you have one or two biggies that you'll want to work on first. You might find yourself saying about one particular thing, 'I really want to stop this *now*.' That's great if you're homing in on what's really important, but if you're phrasing it this way in your head, you're focusing on what you *don't* want rather than on what you *do* want. To help you find what you really want, imagine what you would be doing instead if you stopped or changed this one thing. How would you spend the time you once spent on the habit you want to break? How would you feel and what would you want to do? Thinking about this should help you see where you really want to go; what you want to head towards, rather than what you want to move away from.

So, go on. Write down those thoughts, and get really clear about what's most important for you to work on right now. . .

Well, have you written those ideas down? I'm not suggesting it just because it helps you to be organised or makes sure you don't forget what you were thinking about, although it certainly does those things. It's important because writing helps to clarify and process our thoughts and has actually been shown to make a big difference to our chances of achieving our goals.

Let's take a look at some research (first some nonsense, then some good stuff!) which shows the impact that writing down goals can have on whether we achieve them or not.

Dr Gail Matthews carried out some research in 2001 into the effectiveness of written goals compared to goals that were just thought about. She had discovered that a 'well-known study' of a graduating class of Harvard students in 1953 (in some cases they were referred to as Yale students) was actually an urban myth. You might have heard of it. The study supposedly found that just 3% of the students had written goals for what they were aiming to achieve after graduation. The other 97% either had no clear plans, or had thought about their goals but hadn't written them down. Twenty years later, it was said, the 3% who had written down their goals were earning the same as the other 97% put together.

When she discovered that this research had never taken place, Dr Matthews felt compelled to carry out a real study into how goal achievement is influenced by, among other things, writing down goals.

Her study involved 150 people ranging from twenty-three to seventy-two years old. 25% were men, 75% women, and they came from a wide range of different backgrounds and professions. They were split randomly into five groups, and were all asked to think about goals they hoped to achieve, or wanted to work towards, over the next four weeks:

- **Group 1** were asked to just think about their goals.

- **Group 2** were asked to write their goals down and give ratings for various aspects of the goals.

- **Group 3** were asked to do the same as Group 2, but also to write down some actions that they were going to commit to, in order to achieve their goals.

- **Group 4** were asked to do the same as Group 3, but to send those action commitments to a supportive friend.

- **Group 5** were asked to do the same as Group 4, but also to send a regular progress report to that supportive friend.

At the end of the four weeks, two significant findings emerged. Firstly, *all* of the groups who had written their goals down had achieved significantly more than the group that had only thought about their goals. In fact, just the act of writing down goals appeared to make it 50% more likely that those goals would be achieved. Secondly, Group 5 (those who had to send regular progress reports) achieved significantly more than all of the other groups.[4]

I'd really like you to keep both of those findings in mind as you move on, so you can put into place whatever will help you achieve the goals you set yourself. From a purely practical point of view, if you write your thoughts and ideas down then you'll have something to refer back to when you're doing the exercises that lie ahead rather than having to recall the details each time.

Read through that list you've made (I *have* persuaded you to write it out now, haven't I?).

By now, you should be clear about which areas of your life you want to focus on, and what needs to change to get that temperature going up. Let's delve a little deeper.

---

4   Forbes Books, 'The science behind setting goals (and achieving them)', Forbes Books (18 July 2017), https://books.forbes.com/author-articles/the-science-behind-setting-goals-and-achieving-them, accessed 8 June 2023

Tell me what you want – no, what you *really* want!

That list you've made probably reads like a set of goals. Maybe you wish you could be healthier and trimmer, or that you had more money. Maybe you wish you had a better social life, or more time to yourself. Do you feel that if you just had a better job, or relationship, or went to the gym more, or could stop shouting at the kids so much, or spent more time meditating, or less time on housework, or didn't work so hard, or had an expensive new car then everything would be fine? Notice how some of these are actually statements of what you don't want.

If you find yourself coming up with phrases that say what you want to stop, or what you want less of, and you're having trouble turning those phrases around into positive statements about what you want, try thinking to yourself, 'OK, if I *didn't* have or do that thing, what would I have or do instead?' For example, if you don't shout so much at the kids, what would you do instead, and what would that give you? A calmer family life? Perhaps what you really want is to be a calm, positive and assertive parent? Or a better role model for your children? Write that down rather than, 'I want to stop shouting at the kids so much.'

In a standard goal setting exercise, you would decide what you want, work out what you need to do to get it, put together an action plan and try to have some kind of regular progress-check in place to try to keep you on track. That's fine as far as it goes, but there are two key problems with that approach:

First, it relies totally on a conscious process and does nothing to engage the unconscious mind, so breaking old, destructive habits and making new, better ones is going to be hard going. Second, it accepts the initial goal you decide upon without question, but most of the time the goals we first come up with aren't what we *really* want.

We've talked about the first point before, and that's where the work we'll be doing to get your unconscious mind on board will make a huge difference. Right now, I want to look at the second point. You might be thinking, 'Who do you think you are to suggest that I don't know what I want?' but bear with me.

Those goals you've set are just a surface layer of targets that you can understand clearly and aim for. When we set ourselves goals like these, it's more significant to work out what lies behind them. What will you *really* be getting if you achieve this goal? For example, if one of your goals is to earn more money, ask yourself why you want more money:

- Do you see it as a way to feel more secure or safe?

- Do you think it'll create a happier family?

- Will it make you feel successful?

- Will you feel more reliable and responsible as a good provider for your family?

- Will it bring you freedom from worry, as you'll no longer panic when a bill lands on the door mat?

- What do you plan to do with that extra money?

It's in the answers to these questions that you'll find what you really want – the *emotion* that you believe having more money will deliver.

If your goal is to run a 5 km race, what makes you really want to do it? Is it to feel you're doing your bit for charity? Is it to feel satisfied that you've bought into an exercise regime that'll make you feel fitter, stronger and younger for longer?

For me, while I'm writing this, one of the things I want to change is that I want to have a super-fit body. I was hit by a car while out on my road bike. As a result, I haven't been able to maintain the fitness levels I want. If I did have that super-fit body, what would that give me? In my case, it would make me feel secure that my health is back on track. I'd feel confident that I was ready for whatever physical challenges I might choose to do; that with a little training, I'd be able to complete events well, feeling healthy, happy and having enjoyed it.

Notice how it's all about feelings. We're all chasing the *emotions* we want, not the *things*. That's what drives us. The feelings we experience are far more important than the goals we're aiming for. Those goals are just useful stepping stones that we can use to get where we want to be. Everyone has at least one emotion that they feel they don't have enough of, and we need to discover what that is for you.

It's easy to assume that what's motivating someone (yourself or others) is the obvious, surface goal. However, if you take a little time to figure out what's really behind that goal, it can be surprising and can sometimes even resolve problems all by itself. I can clearly remember the first time I realised that the apparent motivation isn't always what's behind someone's actions.

I'd not long been working for Estée Lauder. I was nineteen, and I was about to go on holiday for the first time with my boyfriend, John Carroll. We were heading off to Cyprus for two weeks, and I was really excited about it. I still lived at home with my parents and my younger brother Glynn and little sis Rebecca. Every Friday night I would hand £10 to my dad in a kind of ritual at the dinner table. It was my contribution towards my board and lodging, and was part of learning to be more grown up and setting a good example for Glynn and Rebecca. I was only earning about £90 per week back then, so £10 a week was what my parents had agreed I should give them.

But this Friday night was supposed to be different. I was heading off to Cyprus the next morning. I'd worked really hard and saved a lot of my money to be able to pay for the flights and accommodation for the holiday, and to have a bit of spending money while I was there. I really didn't have any spare money.

At dinner that night, Dad asked if he could have my board money. I was a bit surprised and asked what he was talking about. They weren't going to have any washing or ironing to do; I wouldn't be eating any of their food, or using any electricity. Basically, I just wasn't going to be there. What was he thinking? He must be joking, right? Wrong.

'That's not really how it works, love,' my dad said.

'If you were renting an apartment somewhere, you couldn't just ring up the landlord and say, "I'm sorry, but I'm going on holiday for the next two weeks, so I won't be paying rent for the time I'm away." And you certainly couldn't give the bank manager a call and say that you're not going to be paying your mortgage for a couple of weeks. As it happens, you live here with me and Mum and the kids, and you've got access to everything whenever you like, so whether you're actually here or not, you still have to pay your board.

In fact, I'll need £20 to cover the two weeks – not just the £10 for this week.'

Well, at that point, I just lost the plot. £20 was a lot of money for me right then. There were things I really wanted that I could have bought with that money, and it could certainly have paid for several meals out when I was in Cyprus. I just couldn't believe he was expecting me to pay this money when I wasn't even going to be here! I made it clear in no uncertain terms just how outrageous I thought my parents were being, then slammed down my knife and fork (looking daggers at my little brother who was happily insisting that, of course, I had to pay up) and stormed out of the house with a great deal of banging of doors (nineteen-year-olds are good at that kind of thing). I jumped into my little 'Doris the Daf' car and with a hiss and a roar we hurtled out of the drive spraying stones everywhere and doing nothing to hide just exactly what I felt about the situation. I went straight over to John's house and poured it all out to him.

By the time I'd finished, we'd both concluded that my parents' attitude was absolutely appalling. It was clearly time for me to make a stand. We agreed that when we came back from holiday that we would look for an apartment together. I don't think either of us had much idea of what that would cost, but it had to be better than living under such unreasonable rules, surely?

All I was focused on at the time was the money. It seemed to me that all that mattered to my parents was getting that £20 from me. Of course, there was far more behind that request for board money than a desire on their part to have an extra £20 while I was away. To Mum and Dad, it was about preparing me for real life, about helping me to grow up and take responsibility, about teaching me to manage my finances the way I would need to when I was out in the world on my own.

It must have been so difficult for my parents that night, trying to work out what they should do. What *do* you do when your nineteen-year-old daughter has stormed out of the house and is flying off to Cyprus the next day and you won't see her for two weeks, and it's all over a measly £20?

Well, my amazing parents did as good a job with this situation as they had done so often before, and I'll never forget how they decided to handle it.

When I eventually came back home that night (as they knew I would, because all my packing and passports and holiday stuff was still at home), it was close to midnight. The house was in darkness, and everything was silent as I slipped quietly past our lovely Jack Russell dog, Tinker, curled up asleep in his basket, and creaked my way up the stairs to my room in the attic. I was still fuming about the whole thing and couldn't wait to get my stuff together and leave in the morning.

When I got into my bedroom, there was an envelope carefully placed on my pillow, with the words 'Room for Rent' handwritten on the outside. I couldn't believe what I was seeing.

'They're going to rent my room out to someone else!' I thought. 'And they're making sure I see the advert before I go away just to spite me. They're actually going to kick me out when I get back from holiday, just because of this £20!' I was absolutely appalled, but curiosity got the better of me. I opened the envelope and took out the note inside. As I read it, I felt my anger dissolving. This is what the note said:

ROOM FOR RENT

All washing and ironing done for you

All food prepared and cooked for you

Barbecues

Birthday celebrations

Christmases

Holidays

Space freely available for friends to stay over

Brother and sister included for you to love, boss around or ignore depending on your mood and theirs

Friendly dog to play with

A shoulder to cry on

Someone to listen to you whenever you need them to

Good advice if you want it

And always, always love unconditionally

All for just £10 per week

Well, you can imagine: by the time I reached the end of the letter, I had a huge lump in my throat and the tears were running down my face. What they'd done was point out what was underlying, what all this was really about. To them, way more important than the £20 was the lesson they were trying to teach me. The lesson that you can't always have everything your own way; that you can't have your cake and eat it; that you shouldn't take things and people for granted, however close they might be; the lesson about taking responsibility and accepting that to prepare you well for life and to do their best for you, loving parents might sometimes seem unreasonable to an inexperienced nineteen-year-old.

It was a perfect way to defuse the situation. I went to my parents' room where they were both sitting up in bed with a cup of tea, waiting to see what effect their note might have.

I apologised and gave them the £20, saying that I hadn't really understood what it was all about. I said that of course I would manage with a bit less spending money; that I realised I should have made sure that I had enough to pay my rent as well as to go on holiday.

It would have been far easier for them not to have bothered about the rent money, but it was more important to them to guide me and prepare me for real life. I realised that the emotions behind their request for the rent money were actually based in absolute love, support and guidance.

So off I went to Cyprus the next day, feeling poorer, but happier. When I unpacked my suitcase, what did I find but an envelope with £10 in it from my parents and a note saying:

> Have a wonderful time – here's a little extra spending money. Enjoy! Looking forward to hearing all about it when you get back.
>
> Love from Mum and Dad

The fact that this envelope must have been in my suitcase before we'd even had the argument about the rent money just made it clear that, for them, it had never been about the cash.

What I'm trying to say here is, don't be blinded by the concrete goals you set yourself. Dig down and discover the *emotions* you're really looking for. It's the emotion behind any goal that provides inspiration and motivation. That's why if you can identify it, and work out what you're *really* after, you're far, far more likely to achieve what you want. Knowing what you really want releases you to be flexible and creative about the routes you might take to get there.

What have you been doing until now?

Hopefully you've now got an idea of what you want to feel when certain aspects of your life are on track. You might also be a bit clearer about the emotions you're really looking for. When you read over your list of the things you want to change, you'll almost certainly see some things that you've been unhappy with for a long time. Why haven't you done something about them already? Why don't you already have those feelings that you want? If you've had them in the past, what happened? Where did they go?

It can be difficult to understand how and why things go wrong. You know you do want to change, and you can't understand why you keep failing. You know this 'problem' is holding you back in some way, yet you don't seem to be able to keep motivated about doing the things you know will make a difference, no matter how much you think you want to. You know you're sabotaging your own attempts at success, and yet you just can't stop the same destructive habits from taking control again and again.

Believe me; I know what it feels like to be in that place. The most significant time this happened was when I was doing a bit of modelling. That sounds glamorous, doesn't it? I thought so at the time, too! When I was seventeen and still at school I signed myself up with a modelling agency in Manchester. The principal of the agency, Mavis Roper (who is a good friend to this day), suggested that I needed to lose a couple of stones if I wanted to be a successful model. She told me to come back and see her if and when I had lost the weight.

I had a chat about it with our lovely family GP. I told him what Mavis had said, and how important it was that I lost this extra weight. I wanted to lose the weight within two months. I'd worked out that if I ate no more than about 1,000 calories a day, I could just about make it, but I wanted to run it past him first. Was this something we could do? He, of course, said no. It wasn't a sensible or healthy way to go about it. I knew there was a product called the Cambridge Diet, which involved having drinks instead of breakfast and lunch, the odd diet bar during the day, and then having a fairly normal meal with the family in the evening. I decided in my adolescent wisdom that this was the best way to get what I wanted. Ignoring the advice of my GP and my mum, I embarked on two months of this regime. It may not have been sensible or healthy, but sure enough, I lost 13 kg (28 pounds) in two months, just as I had planned.

Feeling slim and extremely pleased with myself, I went back to the modelling agency and Mavis was gob-smacked that I was there in front of her again already, having lost the weight so quickly.

Just as she'd predicted, I started to get modelling work – fashion shows and photo shoots – which was distracting for a seventeen-year-old who was meant to be studying for her A levels. It's not surprising that I failed my English Literature A level. I wasn't too concerned, because I had just won a contract to go and do some modelling in Japan. There were about 160 girls on the agency's books at the time, and the agent from Japan was only picking six models to go over and do a season in Tokyo. Being picked for that assignment, I felt that I was really on my way! Who needed A levels when they had a glittering career as a successful model ahead of them?

Off I went, now eighteen years old, to spend four months in Japan. I had no money – only what I earned from the modelling. 60% of that went to the agent to pay for board and lodgings, and almost every penny of the remaining 40% went to pay off my air fares. I really didn't see any money for a long time. I was literally surviving hand to mouth on what my parents managed to send through. Tokyo was so expensive! Paying for food was a real problem. I remember that an apple cost the equivalent of £7 (the kind of apple you eat, not email on). The cheapest solution that allowed me to eat anything much was McDonalds, so that's what I lived on. By the time the contract was coming to an end, surprise, surprise, I had put all that weight back on.

I arrived back in Manchester, having left a suitcase of my 'slim' clothes with some of my modelling friends in Tokyo. I was hell-bent on getting my weight back down and getting straight back into the modelling again – or I thought I was. However, something strange was happening. Basically, I had deprived my body for two months by only drinking those low-calorie drinks and putting my body out of balance. Then I'd gone to the opposite extreme by feeding it only empty, high-fat foods for four months. No wonder things were going wrong. After being so disciplined for those first two months, I now couldn't control my eating at all. I knew I wanted to lose the weight again – I *had* to if I wanted to maintain a modelling career – but instead, I was eating more and more of the wrong things. I would eat them secretly and feel awful about it. I would eat four or five chocolate bars in one go as long as there was nobody around to see. I did some part-time work in a taxi office some evenings, as a controller. My eating was so out of control by then that I could merrily eat my way through the whole stock of the Kit Kat machine in the office over the course of one shift.

The modelling agency was, of course, finding it more and more difficult to get work for me. I hadn't just put the weight back on – I had gone way past my original 70 kg (154 lbs) and I was still growing! The final straw was the last job I ever did for them. It was with Great Universal Stores, a Manchester based mail order catalogue. I was being asked to do a week's shoot for them. It was a good job, with pretty good money. I was told it was a 'young mother' shoot, which was great. I would be working with kids, which I always really enjoyed. When I was with the stylist getting hair and makeup done, I asked where the kids were, as everything seemed pretty quiet. You can imagine how I felt when she replied that there weren't any kids involved on the shoot. This was for the maternity wear section!

I was absolutely devastated. No longer could I fool myself into thinking I was a slim, glamorous model. I realised that the idea of a long career in modelling was crashing down around me. Yet, in spite of my world falling apart because of it, I still couldn't control my eating.

Fortunately, I then got the job with the Estée Lauder Corporation, which was going to propel me in a completely new direction. However, there was still the issue of overeating to deal with. I had to wait for a uniform to be specially ordered as they didn't have one in stock that was big enough for me.

I find it interesting that the new, exciting start and inspiring environment didn't create any change in my behaviour. The overeating continued until I made some dramatic changes. I'll go into the how and why of those changes later in the book, but for now, all that matters is that there *is* a happy ending. I'm now a comfortable, healthy size ten-twelve and fitter than most other people at the age of forty-four. Being healthy and active has been an integral part of my lifestyle for many years now, all because of changes I made around that time. The key to it was when I realised that I had to change what was going on in my head before anything else would fall into place.

And that's what you're about to do – you're going to change what's been going on in your head, and start building more positive habits that will transform the areas of your life that you're unhappy with.

It's time to make a note of the things in the past that have stopped you from getting what you want long-term. Use your notebook or there's a useful PDF on the website that you might find helpful called 'Roadblocks'.

Roadblocks (PDF)
https://tinyurl.com/neuralcoding

Think around the things that have blocked your progress before now. Think about the patterns and cycles that you tend to get stuck in. I'm sure you've tried to change these fundamental things before now, so what are the circumstances, people or environments that have stopped you? What things have got in your way and made it difficult to achieve what you want? Too much pressure at work? Disapproval of the people around you? Has illness hampered you? Has someone let you down? Cheated on you? Has your fear of failure or of success made you too afraid to really try?

Maybe your own thought processes have worked against you. Think about the self-defeating things you've said to yourself. Everyone has an internal dialogue. In Neural Coding, we call it Auditory Digital. What tone of voice does yours use? Whose voice is it that you hear in your head? Is it supportive? Negative?

Have you told yourself, 'What's the point? Here I go again, I'll never be able to, I'm not good enough, I'm just not that kind of person, I've just got big bones,' or, 'It runs in the family'? The list could go on and on.

Write down your roadblocks and ask yourself:

- What can you do now/tomorrow?

- What will that first step be and when will you do it?

Have you got it all down? It doesn't matter if it's just some scribbled words – it's only you that needs to know what those notes mean. Make sure you've made a note of those negative self-talks, too. Well done. It's not always easy to be totally honest with yourself. The more honest you are about where you are now and what's holding you back, the clearer you are about what needs to change.

It's all about taking responsibility for where you are now. If you can accept that the way your life is has not been done *to* you, but rather that it's a result of all your conscious and unconscious choices, then you can take back control of it. If you're blaming others for where you are, then you're stuck with it – you can't 'un-choose' anything about that. You're allowing *them* (your past, your family, your genetics. . .) to control who and how you are, and what kind of life you're allowed to have. You're stuck because you're choosing to be a victim rather than a victor.

Even if you don't yet truly believe that you're responsible, it's useful to at least pretend that you do. This creates a sense of freedom and control that allows you to really start making changes.

I recently worked with a client who had been raped when she was younger. She had received counselling and had attended victim support groups to try to get past it, yet years on, she was still stuck where she had been ever since the event.

When I suggested that she could take responsibility for what had happened, you can imagine her reaction. She was both horrified and angry.

'But I didn't *choose* this! He did it to me. He's totally responsible for what happened.'

I asked her to think of it this way. For as long as she pushes the responsibility outside herself, she limits her own choices. By seeing herself as a helpless victim, she would remain stuck. I wasn't asking her to think that it was her *fault* that she had been raped. It wasn't about her taking the blame. I was asking her to take responsibility for how she chose to *react* to the situation and how to *feel* about it from that point on.

If she could accept responsibility for her life, and could accept that all her unconscious and conscious choices over the years had brought her to the point she had reached now, then there was no reason why she couldn't simply choose to no longer be a victim. This would open up so many more choices and experiences for her, not least of which was the choice to get better. And that's what she did. She felt so relieved at the feeling of freedom that came from accepting responsibility. As Eleanor Roosevelt once said, 'No one can make you feel inferior without your consent.'[5] Clever lady.

Take a moment to think what your life will be like if nothing changes. Imagine yourself two years from now, then five years from now. . . Even ten years from now. What will your life be like if you don't change anything? Focus on those things you know need to change if your life is going to get a better score out of ten. Think of how long you've been unhappy with this aspect of your life. Picture the same unfulfilled, empty feeling stretching endlessly and hopelessly into the future. How does it feel? What does your life look like? Are you still blaming others, the situation or the family DNA? Are you still giving all your control away?

OK – enough misery! Change it all round now. Stand up, stretch and take a look out of the window. Notice

---

5   https://quoteinvestigator.com/2012/04/30/no-one-inferior, accessed 2 June 2023

something new, something you haven't noticed before. Great.

So, let's look at a brighter picture. Imagine that those things you know need to change are transformed, starting today. What if you started to feel those emotions you need right now? What would you feel in two years', then five years' time if you could look back having spent all that time feeling the way you've dreamed of feeling?

Imagine going forwards ten years from now with those emotions you want having been fulfilled. What things can you see? What can you feel as you sense what life will be like in ten years' time with that emotion you want in place, with that area of your life having scored full marks throughout all of those years? Imagine looking back and remembering that today was the day that the change really began. Think about how much brighter and full of energy this view of your future seems. Feel the excitement stirring as you realise you really can do this – and honestly, you really can!

It's not just a pipe-dream. You *need* these emotions in your life, and you can use all the tools we'll explore to create them, starting today. We'll use them to change things profoundly and to make those changes stick.

The SCORE exercise

SCORE is an exercise that's designed to help you get really clear and focused about your goals and about what really matters to you right now.

Although I've described the exercise below, to get the most out of it and take advantage of all the resources I've made available for you, I'd really like you to log on to the website, where we've recorded a great video to walk you through it personally. It takes less than ten minutes. It really helps you to get clear on what you want and just what it'll feel like when you've got it.

It's an NLP technique written by Robert Dilts.[6] I first experienced it at an NLP seminar in Auckland, where the guy leading the session was a lecturer in business studies at the university. He was also an NLP Master Practitioner and he loved this technique. He told us he used it a lot, and with great success, with senior business people. I loved it too, and I've used it many times now with my own clients. I've made a few modifications to it and fine-tuned it to reflect what I've found works best for most people.

Before you start the SCORE exercise, you'll need to get a couple of items together. If you go to the website, you will see the SCORE PDF.

---

6   SkillsYouNeed, 'Dilts' Logical Levels' (nd), www.skillsyouneed. com/lead/logical-levels.html, accessed 2 June 2023

SCORE (PDFs) and Notes from SCORE (PDF)
https://tinyurl.com/neuralcoding

It has five cards: Situation, Cause, Outcome, Resources and Ecology, with a corresponding letter to stick on the reverse of each. (Alternatively, you could use five sticky notes. On the first sticky note, write a large 'S'. The next note needs to have a large 'C' and so on, until you have all the letters of 'SCORE' on the sticky notes.) The second PDF is called 'Notes from SCORE'. It's a good idea to have this or your notebook handy to make a few notes as you work through the exercise.

You will also need a piece of string about two or three metres long.

If you've decided there's more than one thing that really needs changing, then take a minute to decide which is the most important. Which is the real big-gie that you know will make the greatest difference, and will motivate you to transform the rest of your life once you've sorted it out? That's the one to focus on while you do the SCORE exercise. You can easily repeat the exercise later for each of the other problems you want to tackle.

You'll find the video for the SCORE exercise here:

SCORE (video)
https://tinyurl.com/neuralcoding

THE SCORE EXERCISE

Take your piece of string and lay it out on the floor in a straight line. Imagine that this piece of string represents your life. Decide where on the string the beginning would be and where the end would be. The length of the string doesn't reflect the probable length of your life – it's just a useful metaphor. Once you've decided which end is which, I'd like you to stand where 'now' would be on the string.

While you're standing in 'now', think about the particular issue that you want to resolve; what's the problem that you have right now that you know, once resolved, will give you a clear path towards your goal?

Where would it be on the string? Alternatively, you might be in the middle of the situation right now. Perhaps it's a situation in the recent or distant past that you feel needs to be dealt with so that you can move on.

Wherever you've decided this problem belongs, take the 'S' for 'Situation' label and place it on the string at the appropriate point.

Now step back from the string and think for a moment about the cause of this problem. How did it happen? How did you find yourself in this situation? Where does the cause lie on the timeline? Really think about it for a minute. Sometimes we assume we know the cause of something, but a little more thought will clarify where the root cause really lies. When you're clear about the cause of the issue you want to resolve, place the 'C' for 'Cause' label on the string at the right point in time.

The next thing to think about is 'O' for 'Outcome'. When would you like to achieve the desired outcome? When do you want to have resolved this issue, or achieved this goal? Place the 'O' label in the appropriate place on your string timeline.

Now what I'd like you to do is stand on the timeline at the 'S', as if you are standing in this situation. Close your eyes. Focus on what you see when you're in this situation; think about what you hear, including the kind of things you say to yourself. Connect with how you feel in this situation and notice where it is in your body. If 10 is intense and 1 is weak, what number would you use to rate it? You'd know if that changed, wouldn't you?

Now I'd like you to go and stand at the end of your piece of string. Remember, this is just a metaphor for your life, so whatever age you feel the end of the string represents doesn't matter. Just know that at this point you're in the twilight years, looking back gratefully over a long and fulfilling life. Picture yourself sitting in a comfortable chair somewhere, perhaps on a deck or terrace or in front of a warm fire, looking out at a beautiful sunset or gazing softly into the flickering flames. You're comfortable and warm, and you feel safe. You feel the peace and wisdom of the years resting gently on you.

As you look back over your life, you remember the particular situation you're looking at in this exercise. You remember the younger you, way back then, dealing with it. As you think about it with the perspective of the years now passed, you think to yourself, 'If I had known then what I know now, this is the advice I would have given myself. . .' Allow a piece of advice or a suggestion to come to your mind. What would it be? What advice would you give your younger self, all those years ago in that situation? Say it out loud to yourself.

(You might want to grab that pen and notebook and make a quick note of the advice you just received – whether you liked it or not! Chances are that you recognise the wisdom in it.)

Now, stepping back from the string, go and stand on the 'O' and close your eyes. Imagine how it would feel to have achieved the outcome you're aiming for. Again, focus on what you would see. Be clear about what you will see that will let you know that you've got the desired outcome. What would you hear? Both externally and what you will be saying to yourself. Hear those things now. Feel what you know you'll feel when this outcome has been achieved. Take a few minutes to really get a picture of it. Be in tune with what it feels like when you're there. Notice where in your body you can feel this emotion of success. It feels good, doesn't it?

Step back off the 'O' now, stepping away from the string.

You'll notice that you've got two sticky notes left. One with 'R' on it and one with 'E'. The 'R' stands for 'Resources'. What I'd like you to do now is to think to yourself, when will you have accessed and made use of all the resources you need to achieve the outcome you're looking for? And also, what resources might you use that you hadn't even thought of yet? What resources are there around you that you haven't tapped into yet? Scribble quickly on that piece of paper any resources you have available to you, any resources that you think might help you to achieve your outcome. You might include particular people, organisations, your own personal strengths, books, money, the Internet, the readers' website that we have for you, with all the resources and tools there, as well as the reading list at the back of this book. Then place the 'R' down on the string to stand for the time by which you aim to have really made use of all the resources you can to achieve your goal.

Step off the string now, and just think for a moment about achieving that outcome. It's good to know that when you've achieved what you want to achieve, you'll experience those feelings you need.

Now look at the last remaining letter: 'E'. It stands for both 'Ecology' and 'Exit'. It's important to think about how achieving your goal might impact those around you. That's the Ecology part. A question for you now is, can you think of a way in which having achieved this outcome would have a negative effect on anybody – yourself or others – at some time in the future?

If the answer is 'no', then that's great, you're all set. If the answer is 'yes', relax – when we come to look at the SPECIFY model, which is up next, we'll look in much more detail at the Ecology side of things and you'll be able to work this through and sort it out. At that point, if you want to, you can come back to SCORE and look at it again. Either way, you can now take the 'E' note, which now stands for Exit, and place it on the timeline at a point that feels appropriate to you. It represents a time when this situation will simply no longer be an issue. The time when you'll be able to feel you've left this situation behind: it's resolved.

Now I'd like you to stand back in the situation and close your eyes again. This time, you have the wise advice, and you know the resources you can call on to help you achieve what you want. How does the situation feel now? Notice how different even your body feels, physically, with this new perspective. Notice how the problems relating to this situation perhaps don't feel so close, or quite so huge. Notice that you now have some ideas about what you need to do. Finally, notice how you now know you can achieve what you want, because you've already felt what it's like to have that outcome and you've given your unconscious mind some suggestions about how you can get there.

It's a simple but surprisingly powerful exercise, and helps you to see your way out of a difficult situation, or towards a desired outcome. Just by taking a bit of time you can work out how to handle things in a way that feels right to you, that feels good and that empowers you.

I remember a difficult situation many years ago, where the SCORE exercise might have come in handy. I was working with Estée Lauder at the time. I'd settled into the job of field training executive, having got over my initial shaky start. We were in the London headquarters preparing for the launch of a new fragrance. In a meeting with the managing director, we were making sure that we'd thought about every eventuality and that everything was in place for a perfect launch. It was to be held just a couple of days later in a prestigious London hotel in Knightsbridge. We'd invited all the general managers and senior buyers from the big retailers throughout the UK. Of course, lots of the press would be there. We really needed to ensure all the preparations were spot on.

In the middle of the meeting, the managing director's PA walked in and said something quietly in his ear. We immediately knew there was a serious problem of some kind, as his face just went white. Then he stood up and announced that nobody was to leave the building. Apparently, half of Fleet Street was camped outside due to some news that had just broken.

We had just signed the model, Liz Hurley, to be the face of Estée Lauder. She was engaged to speak at the press conference we would be holding in the next few days and scheduled to be heavily involved with the launch of the new fragrance. However, news had just broken that her famous boyfriend had just been caught by police in a rather compromising position with a young lady in Los Angeles.

Clearly, this would have had a major impact on Liz Hurley. We now had no idea whether she would come to the press conference or not. The press were in droves outside her house, even flying overhead in helicopters. Of course, they knew she was meant to be speaking at our news conference and they were parking themselves outside our HQ in case she might be in there with us. They clearly hoped to catch a glimpse of her, get some photographs or even a comment from her.

We were all ushered into cars and whisked off to the hotel with strict instructions to say, 'No comment,' to any members of the press, who obviously wanted to talk to anyone who had anything to do with Liz Hurley. She must have been in complete turmoil. In two days' time, there was to be the huge launch with Estée Lauder, an important development in her career.

The morning of the press conference arrived and we'd still heard nothing. About half of the buyers and general managers hadn't bothered turning up, because Liz Hurley was the major attraction. They just assumed that with everything that was going on, she wouldn't be there. The depleted numbers were more than made up for, though, by the press as they hovered around hoping to get some news about Liz.

A colleague and I were chatting and sipping champagne, when he suddenly gasped and dropped his glass. It rolled across the floor and came to a halt right at the feet of Elizabeth Hurley, who had just walked in. Full of composure, she picked up the glass, handed it to my colleague with a kiss on the cheek which made him go bright red, and said with a quiet smile, 'I think this belongs to you.'

She was dressed in a mint green Versace suit, and looked stunning. She mingled and chatted comfortably. In short, she was absolutely charming. After a while, the managing director introduced her and she stood up on the stage, smiling at the audience. With a twinkle in her eyes, she admitted to indulging on the *pain au chocolat* and champagne.

It was a gracious way to get rid of the enormous white elephant in the room. Everyone, of course, was wondering what must be going through her mind about her boyfriend's 'indulgences' and the turmoil she must have been in, but nobody had wanted to actually mention it. Personally, I was really impressed by the way she handled the whole situation.

I'm not saying that in the two days since the news had broken, she'd used the SCORE model, but she had clearly been able to work out that, for her, the right thing to do was to go ahead with the press conference and the launch. It maintained her dignity and integrity, and, of course, meant that she was able to develop her career with Estée Lauder as planned. In fact, she gained such a lot of good press and acted in such an impeccable, professional manner that she was made an official ambassador for the Estée Lauder Corporation. Leonard Lauder also doubled her salary, possibly due, at least in part, to the way she handled this difficult situation when nobody would have blamed her for just wanting to lie low and hide until it had all blown over.

Ironically, the fragrance was called Estée Lauder 'Pleasures'. The launch went off successfully and Liz Hurley went on to have a long and successful career with the corporation.

Quite simply, she had a choice. She could either have stayed stuck in the problem she was dealing with, or found her way out of it. She chose to take control, and take responsibility. She found a way to clarify her thoughts, and make sound decisions that enabled her to move forwards. In many ways, that's what the SCORE exercise lets you do. It helps you to take control, to see what resources you have, and to understand what you might have to do to get to where you want to be. It also helps you to access the kind of wisdom that supports you in making good choices.

Once you've completed the SCORE exercise, made a note of anything significant that came up, and are pretty clear on the underlying emotion that you really need, you're ready to work with a fantastic new tool called the SPECIFY model. You'll find it in the next chapter.

FOUR

The SPECIFY Model

We're now going to use a tool that will let you make the emotion you've identified more tangible. It will help you to be clear about what needs to happen to achieve the changes you want. The model is called SPECIFY. You'll find some resource sheets on the website to print out and use as often as you like.

SPECIFY model (PDF)
https://tinyurl.com/neuralcoding

SPECIFY is a model developed by Dr Richard Bolstad, and one of the exciting things about it is that it embraces all the wonderful resources of the unconscious mind.[7] This is in contrast to something like the

---

7   R Bolstad, *RESOLVE: A new model of therapy* (Crown House Publishing, 2002)

SMART model, which you may have come across before. The SMART goal setting model has been successful in business for a long time, but it's a purely conscious way of looking at things.

In contrast, SPECIFY is something that literally feels quite magical when you use it. Normal goal setting feels a bit like a daydream: 'One day, when I . . . , then I'll be happy.'

It's always 'one day' or 'someday', but never 'now'. It's too far in the future, always out of reach and we never quite seem to get there. It's time to use something that makes it real, and starts things happening right now. *Today.*

I was introduced to the SPECIFY model in 2008 when I was doing my NLP Master Practitioner course in Auckland. I was just starting to train for a fairly major physical challenge, and without the SPECIFY model, that challenge would have been much more difficult. It's a really powerful, practical model and definitely not one of those things that just remains an interesting theory. In fact, when my business partner, Mike Catton, and I run our award-winning Seize Your Life two-day seminars, the SPECIFY model is one of the core parts of the course. It allows people to understand how to communicate at an unconscious level and to connect with what they truly want.

Let's start by taking a brief look at the SMART model of goal setting that's used so much, and explore why it's just not enough.

This model is a conscious, business-based model; results- and productivity-driven. SMART is a mnemonic (constructed from the initial letters of key words that we want to remember), and there are a few variations of what the letters stand for, but they're all broadly similar:

- S = Specific

- M = Measurable

- A = Achievable

- R = Relative (or Realistic)

- T = Timely (or Time-bound or Timed). In other words, there is a time within which you're aiming to achieve this goal

The SMART model is so heavily conscious that it can easily become boring. Experience has taught me that just working your goal through this model tends to transform it into something unattractive, dull and entirely uninspiring. It doesn't get under your skin or into your senses. It doesn't capture a sense of excitement and drive. It seems superficial and one-dimensional.

In contrast, the SPECIFY model is so much more exciting and motivating to use. It's *not* just another goal setting model. Neural Coding is really the study of excellence, and all we've done with the SPECIFY model is look at the common factors of how great people achieve great things, and then pull it together into a package that makes it accessible. This way, *all of us* can achieve great things, way beyond our wildest dreams.

Let me share an example of what I mean. When I had lost a lot of my excess weight (partially through better eating habits, but also by exercising more), I rediscovered my love of sports. In particular, I started doing more running for charity. I started to take part in marathons, which meant a fair bit of travelling. On one occasion, my husband Keith and I had flown to New York so I could run the New York marathon. On the plane back home, Keith raised the subject of whether we really wanted to keep jumping on long haul flights to run marathons. Couldn't I just run marathons in Portugal?

I explained that there are few marathons in Portugal. 'OK,' he jokingly replied, 'Why don't you just run across Portugal instead?'

Now, he might have been joking, but I thought it was a great idea! So, we started to plan. It would be a huge challenge: the equivalent of running almost a marathon a day for seven days.

We got in touch with Jane Tomlinson, an amazing British woman who you might have heard of. Her response to being diagnosed with terminal cancer in 2001 and being told she probably had about six months to live, was to undertake a series of physical challenges that would have daunted the most fit and healthy of individuals such as marathons, triathlons and Ironman competitions. She cycled from Rome to Leeds, and even all the way across America. Virtually all of these feats were done in constant pain, and while enduring various treatments for her cancer – and yet she was rarely seen without a smile on her face.

At the time that we contacted Jane and her family, she was in the middle of her journey across America. We asked if the Tomlinsons would support us in our venture of doing a big run across Portugal, as we wanted to raise lots of money for charity. Specifically, we wanted half of the money to go to the fantastic charity that Jane did all her challenges for, and the rest to go to a charity called ACCA that does outstanding work with young and vulnerable children and teenagers in Portugal. With Jane and her husband Mike's seal of approval, we were able to raise the profile of what we were doing, and increase the amount of money we could raise for the charities.

It took fifteen months to plan and prepare for the run. Even with the backing of the Tomlinson name, it was still a huge undertaking, with many practical difficulties. For example, the route we were meant to be following included stretches of road that were yet to be built, so a great deal of time was spent planning alternative, safe routes.

And it wasn't just about me and a friend running across Portugal. We wanted to get as many people running with us as possible. Then, with a great running friend called Sue Howard, we set up clinics specifically for ladies over fifty and trained up lots of them to be able to run 10 km sections of the run with us. We also worked with a school to involve and train up children to be able to run the last 10 km of the journey, too.

Sadly, before we had completed the planning and organising of the run, Jane Tomlinson died (six *years*, not six months, after being diagnosed!). By then, she and her brother Luke had raised a phenomenal amount of money for charity: over £1.5 million.

If anything, Jane's death made me even more determined to make this event a success. For someone who had only run the odd marathon (and not in a fast time, I might add!), and who had never organised anything like this, there were times that the whole idea just seemed huge, overwhelming and way too big for me. I had no idea whether my body would hold out for the whole journey, or even if we would manage to get everything organised properly in time.

When I started learning about the SPECIFY model in my NLP Master Practitioner training with Dr Richard Bolstad, I saw how it could really help me – especially the first part of the model. It focuses on getting sensory specific about knowing that you've got what you want. In other words, what will you see, hear and feel that will make it clear that you've achieved your goal? Sound familiar? This is what you did when we looked at the SCORE model, so you've already played with this way of thinking.

Well, I already knew the route we were going to run, particularly the last part of it as I'd cycled it with my close friend, Jill Edwards, who was doing all the route planning. I'd seen exactly what the end of the route looked like, as the road went slightly uphill, with a lighthouse standing proud against the sky at the end. I decided to use that knowledge to picture what the end of the run would be like for me.

I imagined the sun on my back with about fifty metres to go to the end. I imagined seeing the finishing line up ahead. I pictured all my friends and family there, with their smiling, proud faces and lots of other people running along with us, achieving their own personal running goals. I imagined hearing my dad calling out, 'Go on, lass!' and people clapping and cheering, and the pounding of running feet on the ground. I imagined hearing my internal dialogue saying, 'We've really done it! The whole thing! We've raised all that money for charity! We've made it the whole way!' And I could feel what my body would feel like: tired, but euphoric, with a lump in my throat from the emotion of having achieved this – pure delight in every inch of my being.

So, when I was actually doing that run, and we got to the tough middle days when the whole thing seemed endless, and it was hot, and hilly and dusty and so hard, I would call up that image I had created. I would immerse myself in the things I knew I would see, what I would hear and what I would feel when we reached the end. It was so specific and so clear that it helped me enormously. It allowed my unconscious mind to remember exactly what we were working towards, and to do whatever it needed to do to keep me on track. It pulled me through the difficult times, because I really knew I was going to get there.

And, of course, I also kept thinking that, no matter how hard it might seem to me, it was nothing compared to what Jane Tomlinson had regularly put herself through. I was fit and healthy, and yet Jane, who'd always thought of herself as 'an ordinary mum who happened to have cancer', had done this kind of thing and much, much more, while in pain and on medication which makes people feel extremely ill.

And when we started the seventh day of the run, I was really looking forward to that final 10 km. I absolutely knew for certain now that we were going to do it. I had such a clear picture in my mind of how it was going to be. And do you know, apart from the fact that it was cloudy rather than sunny, it was exactly as I'd imagined it. That image had kept me going through the equivalent of seven back-to-back marathons, as well as through the months of preparation and organisation.

What I hope this illustrates is that using the SPECIFY model really can help us achieve quite extraordinary things.

So, think about the goal that you worked through in the SCORE exercise, and now that you're a bit clearer on it, and may have a better idea of the emotions you're hoping it will bring you, let's take it for a workout through SPECIFY.

S is for Sensory Specific

Sensory Specific is a Neural Coding term, and it relates to how you will know that you've got what you want. It's really important to think about what all your senses will experience when you've achieved your aim. Right at that moment when you've got what you want, how will you know that you've made it? What will you see, hear, feel, taste or smell? What will you be saying to yourself? It's important to be extremely specific about it.

Conrad Hilton was once interviewed by a keen, young reporter, who was eager to make a name for himself. He'd carefully done his research, and asked about when Hilton was just a bell boy. However, Hilton is believed to have answered that he was never *just* a bell boy, but he had *always* owned a chain of hotels and needed to figure some things out first.[8]

---

8   G Hoover, 'Conrad Hilton: The dreamer who conquered an industry' (Archbridge Institute, 2018), www.archbridgeinstitute.org/conrad-hilton-the-dreamer-who-conquered-an-industry, accessed 13 June 2023

You see, he always knew he was going to own a chain of hotels. My guess is that he already knew in detail what it would be like. In his mind he could already see the hotels; he could picture lots of people checking in with their expensive baggage; he could hear the noise of the guests chatting at dinner and the smells of wonderful food being served; he could hear the sound of his own inner voice saying, 'You've done it!' My guess is that even when he was 'just' a bell boy, he was already sensory specific about it all.

An important point to make here is about that statement that there was some 'stuff' he had to do first. He didn't expect to have some nice dreams about being a hotel owner, then sit around waiting for it to happen. That would be like hoping you'll win the lottery, but never bothering to buy a ticket. No, he knew that *he* had to take action – and you'll have to take action too if you want things to change. This book isn't some kind of magic wand. It doesn't contain some great secret that you can just read about and then wait for it all to come to you. That's not what living is about!

This book is about taking the tools we know work and actually choosing to use them – *bothering* to take action.

I'll do everything in my power to make it as easy as possible for you, but you'll still have to get out there and do whatever it is you need to do. Fasten your seatbelt and get ready while we look at an amazing guy who demonstrates just how powerful a tool engaging your senses in this way can be.

His name's Lewis Pugh. He's an English maritime lawyer, brought up in both England and South Africa. In 2007, he decided he wanted to raise global awareness regarding the melting of the ice caps. It was something he felt really strongly about, but how could he draw people's attention to the issue?

He decided that if he did a stunt that everybody thought was impossible, it might draw a lot more interest than just standard campaigning would.

So, he decided to swim for 1 km through the North Pole, where the water is, at best, –2 degrees, in just a pair of swimming trunks.

Obviously, his medical team and coach didn't like the idea. In their opinion he could easily lose digits, possibly limbs and even his life. However, Lewis Pugh was absolutely determined, and was convinced he could achieve this because he was sure he could prepare himself better than anyone else thought was possible.

He was already a strong swimmer and extremely fit and healthy. He would make sure he had enough body fat to keep him naturally insulated. The reason he was certain he could do it was because of the *mental* preparation he was going to do every day.

He went ahead and he swam that kilometre. It took him nineteen minutes, which is a pretty good time for a 1 km sea swim. It took him about four months to get full sensation back in his fingers and toes, but he didn't lose any digits and he certainly got the high level of media attention that he'd been aiming for.

In an interview on CNN, he was asked how he had prepared for this seemingly impossible task. He explained that while, of course he'd done all the physical preparation you would expect, it was the mental preparation he had done every day that was by far the most important part of his routine.

He explained how he would sit in his lounge, on the sofa, and imagine he was swimming in the freezing waters of the North Pole.

'I can taste salt water in my mouth. I can hear the sounds of the engines, of Tim Noakes (his coach) screaming at me. I can feel ice burning my skin. I can smell the sea air. I absolutely live that moment. I have swum the North Pole hundreds of times in my mind.'[9]

A fascinating fact is that when he used to sit in his lounge and really live the task, live it in every sense (or in Neural Coding terms, 'fully sensory specifically access' it), his body temperature would actually rise

---

9   M Tutton, 'Lewis Pugh: The human polar bear' (CNN, 2023), https://edition.cnn.com/2009/HEALTH/02/25/lewis.pugh/index.html, accessed 12 June 2023

by 2 degrees and create a feverish state. This happened because, as you now know, the mind doesn't know the difference between something that's real and something that's vividly imagined. It treats them both the same. Notice, too, that he didn't just sit and visualise – he used all of his senses. He heard it, felt it, tasted it and smelled it. Every sense was living through that moment over and over again, until the day he did it for real.

What Lewis Pugh did was use an intense form of *Sensory Specific* preparation. His choice of describing the water as 'burning' his skin rather than freezing was important here. It helped him to interpret the signals he would get in those freezing conditions in a particular way. He was giving his unconscious mind absolutely detailed, specific information so that it knew exactly how to respond when the actual event came around.

Being Sensory Specific is not simply visualising in the way that many sports people do. It means accessing all the senses in a way that supports whatever we're setting out to achieve. Our brain communicates with those five senses, as well as the sixth one, which in Neural Coding we call 'auditory digital' – our internal dialogue, that inner voice that we all have. If we can get all of these senses working in harmony with one common aim, then we're harnessing an exceptionally powerful tool that makes almost anything possible.

And if you're thinking, 'Well, Amanda, that's all well and good, but he was already a powerful swimmer,' or, 'I'm not so sure about this stuff about the brain not knowing the difference between what's real and what's imagined,' then just remember the lemon exercise in Chapter 2. (If you didn't actually do the exercise, I'd urge you to go back now or head to the website and give it a try.) There was no lemon, yet your imagination stimulated a genuine physical response.

If you still need convincing, try to think of a time when you felt totally, absolutely confident. However, you're not allowed to see anything in your mind's eye. You're not allowed to imagine the scene, hear any sounds, smell anything or imagine the feeling in your body at the time. It's really hard, isn't it? It's almost impossible to get a real sense of what it felt like to be confident if you're not allowed to access those senses, even though it's only in your imagination.

But now, thinking about that same time when you felt so confident, really picture it. What could you see, what could you hear and what could you feel that tells you that you were totally confident? What's your inner voice saying to you? What positive thoughts were you having? What could you smell? Maybe a fragrance you were wearing? Or the smell of the country you were in? Maybe there was something you could taste at the time? Champagne? A special meal?

It's so much easier to access those emotions and feelings when we can make use of our senses to transport us back to that experience. In fact, it's impossible to really access any emotion without seeing a picture, hearing something or feeling something in our bodies. Those are the three primary senses that we are using most throughout this book: seeing, hearing and feeling. It's important to remember when we talk about hearing that we mean a combination of external, objective sounds and that internal discussion we have with ourselves most of the time.

So, let's get back to thinking about whatever it is that you're going to change. You've decided what you're going to focus on, and you've worked out what emotion it is that this change is going to deliver for you.

Now, just imagine for a moment what it will be like when you've achieved this goal. It's time to be really sensory specific. Take a minute to start imagining clearly what you would be doing and what your life would be like if you had created the change you're aiming for. What would you see? Take a few minutes to really imagine it vividly. What would you hear? Think about the sounds that you would notice around you, but also, what dialogue would be going on in your head. Finally, what would you feel, both emotionally and physically. Really take a few minutes to imagine this as strongly as you can. Really immerse yourself in the experience. Access in detail what it will feel like when you have achieved that goal.

This sensory specific stuff is really powerful, but it can work both ways. Remember the sticky start to my

Estée Lauder career? I had just been promoted, and I was really nervous. I had to drive a long way, down to Great Yarmouth. I could remember huge journeys down there as a kid, because we used to go there for holidays. We used to bring our pillows and duvets in our big Volvo car so that we could sleep on the way down. Here I was, only ever having driven short, local journeys and not an experienced driver, but having to drive all that way to run my first training course.

And it wasn't just the long drive that had me feeling nervous. I had to train sixty beauty advisors in this new product called 'Time Zone', a special kind of moisturiser. I knew I was younger than at least half of the audience. It had seemed such a result, getting the job against all the odds. I had been really chuffed that I was the youngest person to get selected for this position, and yet now I was absolutely dreading it.

If I'd known then what I know now, I could have shifted that feeling so easily, but instead, what I did was imagine everything going wrong. The people attending wouldn't want to listen to me. They wouldn't accept what I was saying. They'd be thinking, 'Who does she think she is? She's only been selling for a couple of years and I've been selling for thirty. I'm a top sales person – who's she to be telling me what to do? She's only a young whippersnapper, what does she know?'

This kind of visualisation really wasn't helping. I was creating a movie in my head of the whole thing going wrong. I was seeing boredom, hearing people talking to one another and seeing them rolling their eyes. I was hearing negative, pointed questions deliberately geared to trap me into making mistakes and looking stupid. Or difficult, detailed, technical questions about the ingredients of the product. My stomach was just a mass of knots and butterflies. In fact, I felt physically sick for the entire trip down.

It's not surprising, then, that when I presented that first training session, I did a pretty awful job. I had told my unconscious in specific detail what to expect, and so it delivered exactly that. I hadn't put myself in a resourceful state at all, so my performance was pretty abysmal. My stumbling, mumbling presentations lead to exactly the kind of reactions that I had predicted. It was so bad that I seriously questioned whether I was the right person for the job after all – and I know my boss at the time was having similar doubts about the wisdom of appointing me.

I was actually doing exactly what Lewis Pugh had done in his preparation for swimming the freezing waters of the North Pole, but I was doing it in reverse. I was programming myself for a negative outcome, which was absolutely the opposite of what I was hoping for. There wasn't any room in my mind for the positive stuff because I'd filled it to overflowing with huge, negative images of what I *didn't* want. Most people spend a lot of time and energy feeding their brain with loads of information about what they *don't* want. They dwell on, and run a movie of, all the ways a situation might go wrong. They get sensory specific about it, and make it far more likely that they'll get what they don't want, because they're only letting their unconscious mind see the negative outcome rather than the desired one. Let's not forget: the unconscious mind doesn't process negatives, so it gets right on with helping you to achieve exactly what you want to avoid.

The good news is that it shows that everyone is capable of influencing their unconscious mind. We all do it. We've all had a situation where we've imagined it all being a disaster – for example, sitting an exam and panicking, thinking you won't understand any of the questions, or you'll misinterpret them and write completely the wrong answers. The usual outcome of these pre-exam nerves is your mind going completely blank when you first look at the exam paper. It could be the easiest exam in the world, but at that moment it could be written in a foreign language for all the sense you can make of it. If we're lucky, we usually manage to calm our nerves enough to at least begin to make sense of the questions and understand what we're being asked to do.

So, all I'm asking you to do here is use a skill that you've probably used lots of times before, but to turn it around and use it in a way that will focus your unconscious mind on what you *do* want rather than on what you *don't* want.

Take your goal, the positive change you're focusing on, and imagine it going completely right. Give your unconscious mind all the knowledge and language it needs to understand exactly what you want it to do. Really focus on what you'll see, hear and feel when you've got this thing you really want. Give the physical feeling you expect a size, shape, colour and intensity. That may sound strange, but, for example, you could imagine a successful or excited feeling as a big, round, glowing, yellow bubble of joy. Write down whatever comes to mind in your notebook. Alternatively, you'll find the SPECIFY pdf on the website ready for you to print and fill in as you go. (You might prefer to complete it when you've finished reading this section, whatever works best for you.)

SPECIFY model (PDF)
https://tinyurl.com/neuralcoding

P is for Positive

In Chapter 2, we talked about how the unconscious mind is unable to process negatives. I wonder how often you've focused on what you *don't* want rather than on what you *do* want (for example, not smoking or not eating chocolate cake). This simply leads your mind to think about those things to know not to do them. However, the thought and image of doing them are far more powerful that the second command, which is 'don't do it'! So, make sure that this goal, this aim you're giving yourself, is stated in positive terms.

You need to overcome all that lifelong programming that has happened, because we're generally surrounded by negative commands and statements. Remember the ones we've already discussed? 'Don't run in the corridor / don't dive / don't slip / don't drink and drive / do not enter.'

You need to be bold and think like someone who is extremely certain of what they want. State your goal clearly in the positive, giving the unconscious mind exactly what it needs to be able to support you.

E is for Ecology

Ecology is the study of the consequences and impact that someone or something has on their environment. Let's imagine for a moment that you're in the process of achieving your goal, or that you have already achieved it. Take a little time to consider what the costs or consequences of succeeding really are. Think to yourself, 'When I have X, might there be a situation where it would actually become a problem? When I've completely achieved X, might it have a negative impact on me, or anyone or anything around me?'

It's really important to do this ecology check for two key reasons. Firstly, you don't want to succeed only to find that it causes a major problem in another part of your life which puts you in a worse place than when you started. Secondly, if what you're aiming for is really not a good thing for those around you or for yourself, then you probably won't be able to achieve it. For example, if somebody's goal is to earn X amount of money, but the only way they can do it is to spend so many hours working that they'll have little time for family and friends, the reality is that while they'll try to do it, they're unlikely to accomplish it because of the pressure they'll start to come under from other factors. Or, perhaps they *will* succeed, but it won't bring them much happiness or fulfilment because of the problems it causes elsewhere.

It's quite possible that when you ask yourself the Ecology question, you'll decide that the answer is yes, there are some negative consequences. This doesn't necessarily mean that you need to abandon or change your goal, but it does mean that you have to consider your priorities and you might decide to have some thoughtful discussions with yourself and anyone else that might be affected.

I found myself in exactly this position once. I'd decided that I really wanted to take part in an ultra-marathon in 2012. To complete it, I was going to have to put in a huge amount of training. I had to consider whether this level of training and dedication would present any problems. Of course, the answer was yes. It would severely curtail the amount of time I could spend with family and friends, and particularly with my husband, Keith.

So, after thinking about it, I sat down with Keith and we had a long talk. Fortunately, he was totally supportive, even though the training would impact us significantly for about six months. We both felt it was worth it, so I could then embrace the training regime knowing that I had his full support, and was careful to maximise the time we *could* spend together. By being aware of the impact my goal would have, we were both prepared and keen to minimise any potential 'fallout'.

It's really vital that you're mindful of who is affected by both your goal, and what you'll have to do to achieve it. Sometimes, just sometimes, you'll come to the conclusion that the price is too high, and you'll have to adjust your goal in light of this.

C is for Choices

This is another powerful and motivating aspect of the SPECIFY model that makes it different to many other models.

The fact is that to be successful, achieving your goals should lead to a distinct increase in the choices that are open to you. Think in terms of what achieving your goal will actually bring you. For example, if your aim is to lose weight, what new choices will you have when you've succeeded? Suddenly, rather than just thinking about being slim for the sake of it, you might find yourself realising that you'd be able to go swimming without feeling embarrassed. You'd be able to take part in activities that, right now, you either wouldn't be seen dead doing or literally wouldn't be physically able to. Your choices would be far wider than they are now. Any goal that's worth putting effort into will open doors and make many more things available to you. If, on the other hand, all we focus on is what we're taking away (for example, not eating the foods you love), then we have little option but to feel deprived and to feel that our choices are being narrowed rather than broadened. That's not a resourceful state. The only choice we're seeing is the one we're removing: the choice to eat what we like.

So, look at your goal again and ask yourself, 'By making this change, what choices will become available to me that I don't have right now? By achieving this goal, what choices will be created for me that I hadn't thought of before?'

I is for Initiated (by you!)

This is a nudge, a reminder that it's nobody else's responsibility to get things underway or to get you where you trying to go. *You're* the one that needs to do this, to get started on this journey. This is *not* about sitting and imagining a cheque coming through the letterbox in two months' time, or just waiting for the Universe to provide. You've got to *do* some stuff.

What is that stuff? What are the first things that you need to do to get moving on this?

Think for a moment about someone you really admire. Someone successful and dynamic. Someone you view as a good, positive role model. Someone you would really like to be like. Once you've decided on someone, think to yourself, 'If this person was going to do what I'm going to do, with the resources that I have available, what would their first action be? What would they do right now?' Just picture them in your position and what action they would take. You can be sure they *would* be taking action and not just sitting back hoping that it'll all work out some day.

This is a really useful little game to play with yourself whenever you're not sure how to tackle something. It doesn't have to be the same person each time. Different role models might be better equipped for different situations. They don't have to be famous or super-successful. You can have your own little board of directors tucked away in your mind. It might be made up of a well-known figure or two, an inspirational teacher, a down-to-earth, honest friend and a wise and loving parent or grandparent – absolutely whoever you choose. All that matters is that you perceive these people to have values and strengths that you rate highly and aspire to develop.

The key thing to grasp is that *you* are the one that's going to make this happen.

F is for First Step

This is an old and tired cliché, but clichés only become clichés because everyone identifies with them and recognises their fundamental truths. This old truth is that the longest, steepest, most difficult or ambitious journey starts with the first step. Take that first step and you're on your way.

So, what's the first, small, positive step that you can take *today*? It could be as simple as going onto the Internet and registering for that run you're thinking of doing, or writing a list of good, nutritious foods you'll buy at the supermarket, or making one quick phone call to get some information you need.

What's your first step going to be? It might just be telling someone what you've committed to. That can be powerful in itself.

Y is for YOU

This is a prompt to think about what you bring to the situation. What resources can you tap into and start to use? What strengths do you have? What have you achieved in the past that helps you believe you can achieve this now? It doesn't just refer to your personal resources. You could find useful information or resources online, read relevant magazines or listen to podcasts – anything that will help you achieve your aims.

One of my most valued resources is the personal development library I've created on my phone. I listen to it in the car or when I'm out running. I'm currently listening to *Getting Things Done: The Art of Stress-free Productivity* by David Allen,[10] and I love taking Wayne Dyer with me when I'm out running – he's great company!

So have a good think about what useful resources you have access to – it could even be as simple as watching a particularly relevant movie. Be creative and have some fun with it!

Book List
https://tinyurl.com/neuralcoding

For some inspiration, visit the website. We've got lots of useful resources and recommendations in the Book List. Some of them might be exactly what you need and right up your street.

Finally, stop to think why *you* really want this. What will you really get from it? And how will you celebrate when you've achieved your aim? Plan it in detail. Imagine you're watching yourself as in a movie of the celebration. Who's there with you?

---

10 D Allen, *Getting Things Done: The art of stress-free productivity* (Piatkus, 17 March 2015)

What are you wearing? What can you see, hear and feel? Think in detail, and when it's really clear, then imagine the screen playing in front of you and watch yourself in the movie. Now, step right into that movie; become the 'you' in that scene. Look through your own eyes and see what you will see, hear what you will hear and feel what you will feel. Wallow in it. Immerse yourself in it. Hear the words you're saying to yourself when you've achieved exactly what you wanted.

It's important to not only communicate to your unconscious mind what needs to be done to achieve the desired outcome, but also how to celebrate once it's achieved.

We're going to come back to these images, sounds and feelings later to fix them into your future, so it's great that you've played with that movie to give your unconscious mind something to work with. Fun, isn't it?

A great example of someone who really made use of this technique is Helen. She was a client of mine for some time. She had been diagnosed with breast cancer, having discovered two tumours, both of which were spreading. She'd been advised to have surgery and chemotherapy, but she just point-blank refused to do either. She was determined to heal herself, and she really believed that the unconscious mind had the power to do that.

She surrounded herself with resources – including particular people – which she believed could support her in her aim to heal herself. She consulted a herbalist, had colonic irrigations and ate only raw foods. She and her partner carried out in-depth research about the best approach regarding food and drink, which lead to her completely cutting out processed foods. She took up Qigong, an ancient Chinese form of physical meditation, which she practised every day. She also wanted to use Neural Coding as one of the resources she could draw on to help her deal with what was happening to her.

I saw Helen on and off for about fifteen months – much longer than I would normally work with any client. However, this was an unusual situation. Whenever I was in Portugal, I would see her about once a week. We worked on all sorts of different things, not just focusing on the tumours. In fact, as well as looking at what she was going through with her cancer, we mainly dealt with the psychological impact of several things that she had experienced long before she had developed it.

One of the things that I strongly encouraged her to do was to be sensory specific about how she would celebrate when she felt that she was getting healthier. She said that when she got her full health back, she would know she was ready to go travelling. She and her partner had decided they would travel the world for about eight months, visiting places they'd always wanted to see. For Helen, the film she played in her mind to help her get through the difficult times was a clear one of standing in the airport, luggage at the ready and her partner smiling at her side while they checked in for their flight to Bali where they were going to watch the women's tennis tournament.

I'm so happy to be able to report that Helen and Coral made that flight. When I took them to the airport, it was wonderful to see Helen smiling and healthy, just as she had imagined. They even had bright pink t-shirts made with their planned destinations on the back and 'Live the Life you Love and Love the Life you Live' on the front.

What's more, they both attended my Neural Coding Practitioner training course in New Zealand because they now want to help others learn about, use and benefit from Neural Coding just as they have.

If you didn't fill it in as you went through this section, download and complete your SPECIFY sheet now or use the formula below to write your plans in your notebook. You can even make an audio recording of them using your smartphone, if you prefer.

SPECIFY model (PDF)
https://tinyurl.com/neuralcoding

You can also listen to me guiding you through the process using the 'SPECIFY Refresher' audio. The aim is to get clear, specific and motivated. Take your time and enjoy designing what you want and what you plan to do. Phrase it in clear, precise language. Let it inspire and excite you. By the time you've finished you should be itching to take action! You have your goal.

 **SPECIFY Refresher (audio)**
https://tinyurl.com/neuralcoding

SPECIFY FORMULA FOR GOAL SETTING

My goal is...

Sensory Specific:

- Describe what you see, hear and feel to know that you have your goal. Get specific. Make sure it is stated in the present tense.

Positive:

- State what you want, not what you don't want.

Ecological:

- Does this work for everyone?
- What are the consequences for other parts of your life when achieving this goal?
- What positive outcome are you getting by not achieving your goal?

Choice Increasing:

- What choices does reaching your goal give you?
- What does having this goal give you more of?

Initiated (by you):

- Describe how you will act and what you will do.

First step identified:

- What can help you in this goal? Ask yourself, 'How can this help me?'

FIVE
Creating New Habits

Have you ever switched the bathroom light on when you know there's a power cut? Yes, we all have, because we're all human. We operate on autopilot most of the time. Welcome to the world of habits.

According to Bruce Lipton, a biochemist who wrote a wonderful book called *The Biology of Belief: Unleashing the power of consciousness, matter & miracles*, it's estimated that around 95% of our behaviour is habitual.[11] As we discussed earlier, habits are controlled at a subconscious level. Somehow, we have to programme ourselves into new habits that become entirely automatic and support our goals. Some habits (such as eating too much cake) take us in the opposite direction

---

11   B Lipton, *The Biology of Belief: Unleashing the power of consciousness, matter & miracles* (Hay House, 7 March 2011)

to our goals, while others (such as regular exercise) move us towards our goals. Both habits serve a need of some kind and are enjoyable once they're established. What you want to do now is choose habits that will take you towards your goals, and make them an everyday part of your life.

That's where our award-winning tools will help you. We call them Your Life Compass and Action Day by Day, and although they can be used independent of each other, their real power is when they're used together. Before you use them, it's important that you have already worked your ideas and goals through the previous exercises so that your focus is clear and your unconscious mind is engaged.

By now, you're pretty definite about what your main goal is. You understand the feelings that this goal will deliver for you, and you have an idea of what you have to do to achieve the goal you've set yourself. Your unconscious mind should be thoroughly primed to support your aims. It's time to start developing the behaviour, habits and actions that will keep you firmly focused on what's really important to you. This will allow you to evaluate your progress and keep you motivated over the weeks ahead.

That word 'evaluate' is important. We know that success equals measurement. After all, to know how you're doing, you need to be able to measure it against where you were, and where you're aiming for. Being able to measure and see your progress in this way is the key to motivation. It constantly gives you the feedback you need to stay on track. Our tools will help you to do just that.

So, where did these award-winning tools come from? There's a website called www.wazokucrowd.com where companies, individuals and organisations pose problems and offer financial incentives for people to come up with solutions. A lot of the problems are scientific, for example, looking for a new kind of paint for a Space Shuttle or answers to environmental or health problems. It's like a giant, global problem-solving and brainstorming website. Experts in their field offer solutions if they have them and the person or organisation that's selected as having the best solution is awarded the prize money and also the rights to use the solution they came up with (along with the company that paid for the problem to be solved, of course).

In 2008, my fellow coach and business partner, Mike Catton, noticed a problem on www.wazokucrowd.com that related to obesity. The question was how to create *long-term* behavioural change in people so that obesity was no longer an issue.

In response, Mike created the tools that I'm sharing with you today. They were selected as the winning solution out of more than 1,800 ideas offered by coaches from around the world. What's great is that they are so simple. That's partly why they won. They were looking for something really practical and manageable that anyone could use.

The tools can be used to create long-term behavioural change in any area, not just obesity, so they've become a centrepiece to the successful two-day courses we run in New Zealand, Portugal and the UK (and coming soon to the US), called 'Seize Your Life'.

Andrea was an attendee at one of these 'Seize Your Life' courses in New Zealand. She had already been on lots of personal development courses, but was still struggling to make the changes she wanted in her life. For about five years, she'd wanted to move to Port Douglas in Australia. She absolutely knew this was where she wanted to be, but every time she thought about it, all she could see were insurmountable obstacles and she was beginning to think it would never happen. The biggest stumbling block was the fact that she was in debt, and she wouldn't be able to leave New Zealand until she had cleared the money she owed.

On the 'Seize Your Life' course, she worked this problem through the exercises and started using the tools we're about to look at. Just three days after the course ended, she had resigned from her job and worked out a way to pay off her debts. After just one month, she was off to live the life she had been struggling to create for five years.

That's how powerful the tools we're using are. They really do help to shift your focus, clarify your thoughts and get things moving. Armed with the key goal that you've been working on, let's take a look.

Your Life Compass

The *Life Compass* provides a daily reminder of your chosen direction in life. It's there to keep you on course by focusing your attention and inspiring you to take actions each day to support your aims. By keeping your goals and desired personality traits at the front of your mind, you're far more likely to spend your day productively and in line with what you really want. You'll find yourself *living* your life, rather than letting it happen to you.

When we regularly remind ourselves of our goals, it changes the way we look at the world. It programmes our unconscious mind to look for things that tie in with those goals, and this leads us to notice different things, think in different ways and make different decisions throughout the day. It makes decision-making throughout the day less challenging, as your inner 'compass' steers you towards your goals.

Yourlife Compass™ SEIZE YOUR LIFE

Name:

My Primary Goal:

My Balanced Perspective Goal:

Resources I Have:

I Am Being:

My Empowering Beliefs:

Yourlife Liveit™
=SUCCESS

www.yourlifeliveit.co.nz

YourlifeCompass™   SEIZE YOUR LIFE

What Makes This Important To Me?

My Mission:

Advice To Self:

Affirmations:

YourlifeLiveit™
~SUCCESS

www.yourlifeliveit.co.nz

You can download a copy of the Your Life Compass from the website or you can use your trusty pen and notebook. The important thing is to actually do this, not just read about it!

Your Life Compass (PDF)
https://tinyurl.com/neuralcoding

Let's take a look at the sections of the Your Life Compass and work through them one at a time.

My primary goal

Having worked through the SPECIFY and SCORE models, you should already know what your primary goal is. In Your Life Compass, write your goal as though you're already there. Try to phrase it in terms of, 'I can see. . . I can hear. . . and I can feel. . . when I am. . .'

For example, if your goal is to spend more time fully engaged with your children, your primary goal might read:

I can see my daughter's happy face smiling up at me; I can hear her giggles and questions; I can feel her hand holding mine or her little body snuggled up against me as we share a story book, and I can feel a warm glow of love and pleasure when I am spending more time fully engaged with her.

Perhaps your goal is to reach a particular weight or size, with the real aim being to feel fit and healthy. This time, your primary goal might look more like this:

I can see myself in the mirror looking fantastic in a new, size twelve outfit; I can hear my own inner voice saying, 'Wow! I look great!' and I can feel the lightness in my body and the ease with which I move when I am fit and healthy.

Whatever your goal, find a way of expressing it in the positive, in the present tense and with regard to what you will see, hear and feel when you've achieved it.

My balanced perspective goal

It's quite possible that you won't have to write any-thing in this section. If your primary goal has *only* positive consequences for you and everyone around you, then there's no need to think about a balanced perspective goal. However, when you were going through the SPECIFY exercise, it's possible that in the Ecology section you realised that pursuing this goal could lead to other problems. You might remember my own issue of entering the Ultra Marathon, and having to consider the impact it could have on my relationships with friends and family, particularly my husband, Keith. This is the kind of thing that you need to think about for the balanced perspective section of the Life Compass.

The balanced perspective goal is a particularly important part of the tool. Having established your primary goal, and especially if you're all fired up about changing your life and really going for it, it's all too easy to become so totally absorbed in that life-changing goal that you fail to guard against the negative consequences until it's too late. Assuming you did have an issue when you worked through the SPECIFY model, you need to ask yourself this question: 'How can I achieve this goal while still being able to. . .?' (Insert a relevant phrase that reflects the issue.)

For example, suppose Andrew's primary goal is to earn £5,000 every month doing something he has a passion for: photography. When he works it through the SPECIFY model, he realises that to do this, he is going to have to put in some really long hours, spend time away from home on assignments and focus hard on his work. This could easily detract from the quality time he has available to spend with his wife and young daughter. He's also concerned that the difficult schedules could interfere with his ability to remain fit.

So, his question would be: 'How can I earn £5,000 per month while staying deeply connected to my family?' The answer to the question asked will vary with every individual and their unique circumstances.

Andrew's response might be to make sure he reads a bedtime story to his daughter two nights a week, cooks a meal once a week to sit down and enjoy with his wife, and gets up extra early to go to the gym three mornings a week.

Whatever your question and whatever your answer, the result should give you a balanced perspective goal which reminds you of the other important parts of your life which may also need to be worked on. Andrew's balanced perspective goal might be:

To earn £5,000 per month through delivering outstanding photography, while making time to enjoy a loving marriage, spend quality time with Emily and maintain a fit and healthy body.

Writing a balanced perspective goal simply reminds us each day that there are other areas of our life which are important to us as well as the primary goal that is our main focus.

Resources I have. . .

In this section, you write down the resources you thought of when you completed the SCORE exercise. Be creative. Think of people, objects and services that might help you in some way: books, the Internet, organisations, your personal resources such as determination or past achievements. Whatever the problem you're trying to solve, you have many more resources available to you than you initially think. Remind yourself of them regularly by noting them down here.

I am being. . .

This section is about turning the normal way we think about our goals on its head. We're all pretty good at knowing what we want to have. Maybe we want £10,000 for something special. The way we tend to think about it is, 'Whenever I have surplus cash, I'll save it, and in time, I'll have that £10,000. Then I'll know I'm financially successful.' But it's easy to then sit back and wait for the odd bit of surplus money to come along, and if you normally don't have any cash left over each week or month, then this way of thinking isn't likely to get you far. We think of this as the 'Have, Do, Be' mentality. When I *Have* (extra money), I'll *Do* something (save it), then I'll *Be* (good with money).

It all becomes so much easier if we turn it round into 'Be, Do, Have'. *Be* (tell yourself, 'I am now good at managing money'), then *Do* something about it (actively find ways to cut back on spending or earn more to generate excess cash which can be saved) and that means you'll soon *Have* (the £10,000).

Similarly, if we want to be fit, we'll often think in terms of, 'If I could just lose a bit of weight, I'd be able to exercise more and then I'll be fit and active.' But it never really gets off the ground, because you're waiting to lose the weight before you really do anything or start taking it seriously. However, if you shift your focus so that you think of yourself as being a fit and active person already, it puts you in the frame of mind to start doing the things a fit and active person does: spending time exercising or getting involved with active pursuits, or even just walking rather than driving, or taking the stairs instead of the elevator. By doing this you'll begin to lose weight and will soon achieve what you wanted.

Thinking back to the Conrad Hilton story, he was always 'being' a hotel owner, whatever his current position was officially. Steven Spielberg, the film director, is another example. He basically took himself off to Universal Studios and helped out as an 'unpaid guest' for three years, but the whole time he was thinking and acting and *being* like a movie director.

Andrea (who struggled to leave New Zealand for Australia until she came on our 'Seize Your Life' course) emailed me soon after the course to tell me how it had completely changed everything for her. She had been on so many personal development courses before, but it was the 'Be, Do, Have' part of our course that really made her thinking finally change. She'd been entirely caught up in the belief that until she paid off her debts, she was going nowhere, which of course was true in a sense. She was totally focused on the fact that she needed the money, and was trapped by the lack of it.

She realised that she was stuck in the 'Have, Do, Be' thinking pattern. She needed to *have* spare money so she could *save* enough to pay off her debt, so she could *be* someone who was moving to a location she believed would give her a much better quality of life. This all relied on her waiting around to get extra cash somehow before she could do anything about changing her situation. She couldn't figure out how on earth she could cut back her spending any further or earn any more money to pay off her debts.

The 'Be, Do, Have' section of the course changed her thinking completely, and instantly. She started to see herself as someone who would soon be moving to Australia. This opened her eyes to new possibilities. If she was moving soon, there was a lot of stuff that she wouldn't be taking with her, so she sold it off – including the car. Previously she would only have sold or got rid of stuff once the whole move was organised and definitely going ahead. By turning her thinking around, and becoming someone who was serious about moving, and moving soon, she was able to raise enough cash to pay off her debts. Of course, the result was that she *did* move soon! It's typical of what happens with 'Be, Do, Have' way of thinking – suddenly you can see new solutions that just wouldn't have occurred to you before.

Once you've adopted 'Be, Do, Have' thinking, it tends to stick with you. Andrea recently contacted me to discuss the next exciting step in her journey. It seems that although moving to Port Douglas did, indeed, bring about a big improvement in her quality of life, there were certain aspects that didn't quite live up to what she had hoped. She explored a little further afield and discovered a new location which is just idyllic for her. There was no hanging around this time. No agonising. She sorted herself out and moved to the new location immediately.

So, the idea is to *become* the kind of person you want to be – to become that person now, today, from this moment. Think like that kind of person. Do the things that person would do and you'll end up achieving the things you want to achieve.

It can be a good idea to find a picture or photo (or just write down the names) of one or two people you admire and who epitomise the personality traits you want to display. Think of people who really inspire you in a way that's related to your goal. At any time, you can think, 'If this person was in my shoes right now, what would they do, or say?'

To have what you want, what kind of person do you have to be? What qualities do you have to develop? What are the personality traits you desire? Write your thoughts in this section. You might write something like: 'I am a good saver', 'I am an active person', 'I am confident', 'I am loving and thoughtful', or, 'I am calm and assertive'. Find what works for you, and what fits with your desired outcomes.

Make notes, jot down ideas and stick on pictures of the people you aspire to be like and the things you'll be doing to develop the qualities you want. Alternatively, you might want to get a big sheet of paper to pin up somewhere and cover it with your ideas, images and comments.

My empowering beliefs

In this slot, we need to think of a belief or two that will really help us to achieve what we want. It's relatively easy to think of negative beliefs about ourselves. How often have you thought, 'I'm such an idiot!', 'I just can't do it!', 'I'll never be good enough!', 'I'm too fat to. . .', 'I'm too old to. . .', 'I'm just stupid,' or similar thoughts?

Instead, let's simply find beliefs that support you, and, in particular, those that help with the primary goal you're focused on.

Think about those role models we mentioned earlier. People whom you admire, who have some relevance to the goal you've set yourself and the kind of personality traits that you want to adopt. What might they think about themselves that helps them to be the kind of person you look up to? Can you take those beliefs and apply them to yourself?

One of the key things to realise about beliefs is that they don't reflect reality. Beliefs aren't necessarily true; we just think they are. The unconscious mind doesn't question the validity of a belief; it just accepts that it's true, and then goes on the hunt for evidence to support that belief – and it's good at selectively viewing the world and the things that happen to us so that we only notice the things that appear to support our beliefs.

For example, if you believe that you're hopeless with money, you'll not even notice the times when you've managed to save up for something, or have negotiated a really good price for something, or have found a way to earn extra cash, or have stopped yourself from splashing out on something you couldn't really afford. What you *will* notice and remember are the times that demonstrate how hopeless you are with money: the time you ruined a £20 note by leaving it in a pocket and putting it through the wash; the time you bought an expensive pair of shoes when you couldn't really afford it; the fact that you've got far too much on your credit cards and have been paying a huge amount of interest, with little coming off the total bill. Your unconscious mind will carefully encourage you to ignore *any* evidence that your belief might not be true, and focus on the evidence that proves you right.

So, if our beliefs are not based on objective truth, and are actually subjective, why not select beliefs that will empower us as we aim for our goals? Go ahead and think of one or two beliefs that would really help you to be the person you want to be. Think to yourself, 'If I were (confident, wealthy, fit, whatever is relevant), what would I believe about myself?'

For example, you might think, 'If I were a successful, published author, what would I believe about myself?' Your response might be something like, 'I can express myself in creative and original ways,' or, 'I am full of interesting ideas and I really enjoy the act of writing about them.' It all depends on what your goal is. Choose to believe something that is going to support and empower you. What have you got to lose?

Here are some popular empowering beliefs that others have found helpful. You don't have to pick from these, but they might get you thinking:

- I am capable of doing whatever I set my mind to.

- I am worthy of love and respect from myself and others.

- I am a capable, intelligent person.

- I have all the resources I need within me and I know how to use them.

- I am resourceful and resilient.

What makes this important to me?

In this section, I'd like you to write down what this goal will deliver for you that's more important than just achieving the goal itself. Depending on your goal, you might write something like, 'It would make me feel proud, and worthy of respect,' or, 'I'll feel closer to the family,' or, 'I'll have more freedom to do the things

I really want to do,' or, 'I'll be able to join in with any activities I want to without feeling embarrassed.'

This relates to the underlying emotion that is the real reason for your goal, and you should have discovered this when you used the SCORE and SPECIFY models.

My mission

In this section, write a sentence that sums up your life purpose as you see it right now. When we're 'at mission' we do things effortlessly, because it just feels right. We're doing what we're meant to be doing. When you're at mission, everything is congruent. It's who you're supposed to be, it feels like it's why you're here. It all just fits and falls into place. It doesn't feel like a struggle. I'm so fortunate to be at mission in what I do, because it certainly doesn't feel like a job. I've even started calling it my 'Ying Yang Yong', because 'work' just doesn't sound enough like fun to me!

So, what do you think *your* mission is? If you really have no idea, sit back for a moment and think about some people whose life paths you really admire. What is it about them and what they do that impresses you so much? What higher goal seems to underpin what they do?

Think about activities that really excite you. The things you do where you find that you lose yourself in them, not even noticing time passing. Thinking about these people and things might give you an insight into what your own life purpose might be.

And if you're still not sure, then make one up! Create a life purpose that makes sense to you and feels good. Create one that ties in with the things you feel passionate about, and that just feels right. Use it to drive you forwards. You can always refine your 'mission' as you become more aware of its true nature over time.

For a little inspiration, check out the inspirational mission video on the website. It may get those creative juices flowing.

What's Your Mission? (video)
https://tinyurl.com/neuralcoding

Advice to self

This is where you write the advice that the wise, older version of 'you' gave you in the SCORE exercise. Hopefully you remembered to make a note of it! It's useful to have so that you can frequently ask yourself: 'Am I following that advice?'

Affirmations

You probably already know a fair bit about affirmations. You might recall my saying at the beginning of the book that affirmations on their own just aren't enough, and that most people forget about using affirmations after about a week. However, using them within a framework like this is a different matter. They become just one small but useful cog in a bigger machine that's propelling you towards your desired goal.

Perhaps you have some affirmation cards or a book of affirmations and can pick out one or two that seem particularly relevant. Be careful about how you phrase your affirmations. There's definitely merit in using the present tense, but it can be counterproductive if you're not careful. For example, if you tell yourself firmly, 'I am glowing with health,' when you've got a raging bout of flu, your unconscious mind might get confused (So *this* is what healthy feels like? OK, if that's what you want!). On the other hand, saying, 'I am a strong and healthy *person*' is a rather better option, and might suggest to the unconscious mind that as you're a strong and healthy person, this flu bug won't be able to hang around for long.

In general, however, using the present continuous tense is a safer and less ambiguous way of getting the message through. For example, '*I am getting fitter and healthier every day,*' would point you unquestioningly in the right direction, whatever your current state.

If you're not sure what to use here, take a look at the following affirmations for some general ideas. As long as an affirmation feels good to you, and points you towards your goal, it'll do just fine. You can always change it if you stumble across something that resonates more with you. Try to pick ones that just 'feel' right to you and seem to fit with your aspirations:

- Healthy and wealthy is who I am.

- I am a wise and peaceful soul.

- I love my body and my body loves me.

- I am so happy I can't stop smiling.

- I love life and life loves me.

- With every step I get stronger and healthier.

- Every day in every way I'm getting fitter and fitter.

- I am effective, efficient, focused, outstanding!

- Money flows to me quickly and easily.

- I have all the resources I need inside me.

- I take responsibility for what I do.

- I love what I do and do what I love.

- I am proud of who I am.

- My life is full of reasons to smile.

- I am steadily becoming a better, stronger, more impressive person.

- I'm living a long, happy and healthy life.

You'll also find a swish-looking version (if I say so myself) on the website for you to print out.

Your Life Compass (PDF)
https://tinyurl.com/neuralcoding

Using Your Life Compass

You've completed Your Life Compass. There it is, right in front of you: a definition of who you choose to be and where you're heading. What do you do with it now?

You look at it every morning as part of your morning routine and again just before you go to bed. As you view your Compass, take a few minutes to let the words create vivid stories in your mind so you tune in to what it will feel like to have achieved your goals and mastered those personality traits you desire.

There are two secrets to making the Compass really effective. One is daily repetition. The other is emotional intensity. Between them, they help you to reprogramme your mind into a new way of thinking and being. If you like, you could add some social accountability by sharing your Compass with a supportive friend or life partner. This doesn't suit everyone, but a lot of people find that it really does help to keep them on course.

Now that we've got Your Life Compass sorted out, it's time to take some real action. Let's get going!

SIX

Taking Action Every Day

Earlier in the book, I told you how I realised that to lose all the excess weight I was carrying, I had to change what was going on in my head. It was only if I could change my limiting and destructive thought processes that I would get anywhere in my attempts to shed the excess pounds and become a fit and healthy person.

Once I did that, I was able to establish some really positive habits that have stayed with me ever since. This means that I've been able to take a long-term, healthy approach to life that has felt effortless and enjoyable. The tool we're looking at in this chapter is designed to help you do exactly the same in whatever area of your life you're trying to change.

When I started working for Estée Lauder in Rackhams in Bradford, I was still eating at least five or six chocolate bars a day, and continuing to grow in size. By coincidence, I found myself working with someone who had been at school with me. Her name was Yvonne Kershaw, and in fact we had really disliked each other. I thought she was hard and a bit of a rebel, and she thought I was a right little goody-two-shoes. The funny thing is, once we started working with each other and really got to know each other, we became the best of friends and still are to this day. One big difference between us, though, was size. She was extremely slim whereas, of course, I was anything but. In fact, I used to call her the stick insect.

Yvonne decided to organise our own weight loss competition throughout the whole department. It was a bit like WeightWatchers I suppose, before any of us knew WeightWatchers existed. It was run over a four-month period, and everyone who took part paid £1 a week, and got weighed every week in the staff locker room. At the end of the four months the person who lost the most weight would get to keep all the cash that had been paid in. There was no advice or help, just the incentive of the competition. It was up to everyone to decide for themselves what adjustments they had to make to be successful.

Suddenly there was an incentive, a timescale and a requirement to report regularly. I'd had the incentive to lose weight before, but never tied in with a fixed timescale and a need to check in regularly.

I wouldn't say that I actually dieted specifically, but there were certain things that I just stopped doing. I stopped eating the chocolate bars, for one thing. I started to have a proper lunch with the rest of the girls, whereas before, I used to go out on my own to hide the fact that my lunch was a pile of chocolate bars! By default, I started to learn from them what a healthy lunch looked like.

Yvonne and I started to take it in turns to bring in a healthy lunch to share. We might bring in rye crackers with cottage cheese and black pepper, juicy pink grapefruit that we would cut in half and share, and a bag full of wonderful, ripe cherries that we could munch on as much as we liked. We discovered that these healthy foods were actually quite delicious. We didn't feel deprived, because this was the kind of food that we could eat as much as we wanted of. There were so many choices and so many flavours, and we soon learned which healthy foods we really enjoyed eating.

Another thing I did was to note down the little things I was doing and keep a diary of how I was getting on. This meant that I was able to spot the times and situations when I found it most difficult to stick with my plans. Once I was aware of these, I was prepared for them whenever I encountered them.

Needless to say, over the four months I lost more weight than anyone else (well, I had started from the highest base!) and I won the prize money. I was able to buy myself a really nice bikini to take on holiday with my boyfriend John to Cyprus, where I would now be happy to flaunt my new, healthy body.

What's interesting is that I was successful at becoming slimmer and healthier even though I wasn't really focusing on that. I was concentrating on making tiny adjustments to what I did every day, whether it was putting in place just a few healthier habits, or stopping doing one or two of the destructive habits like eating chocolate for lunch. Over that four-month period, slowly, lifelong habits were formed. To this day, if you asked me whether I would prefer a freshly prepared salad with some feta cheese, olive oil and lemon juice, sprinkled with beans and seeds, or a nice big plate of fish and chips, there's absolutely no way I would choose the fish and chips. I wouldn't be being noble, or depriving myself. I would genuinely enjoy the salad more. I honestly believe that the four months of making those minor adjustments each day formed the foundations of my leading a much healthier lifestyle ever since. At the age of forty-four, I completed a 67 km (42 miles) Ultra Marathon, climbing 2,300 metres in ten hours, and I just wouldn't be able to do that kind of thing if I was feeling deprived, or hadn't developed an automatic enjoyment of these good, healthy habits.

It's not as though I went on some monumental diet with a rigid plan to follow. Nor did I sign up to a fanatical fitness regime. I did little things that I thought would help me to lead a cleaner, healthier life, while still enjoying a wide variety of wonderful flavours. It was just a case of making healthier choices and finding ways of enjoying them. Over time, these became habits that have stayed with me for life. If you're thinking, 'This sounds great! Let me get my hands on the same kind of thing so I can start writing this up straight away!' then let's get on with the next tool.

The Action Day by Day checklist helps you to do what I did: to pick just a few, small, constructive changes to apply to your life every day for thirty-one days, so that those changes become an acquired, automatic habit, a natural part of who you have become.

Your Action Day by Day checklist

It's really important to be aware of the fact that the way we spend each and every day contributes to the sum of our lives. The Action Day by Day chart helps keep you on track each day, ensuring that every single day is meaningful, contributing something towards your primary goal, and feeling like it's bringing you another step closer to the life you really want.

Action Day by Day™

Name:

Month/Year:

" How we spend our days is of course how we spend our lives."

SEIZE YOUR LIFE

DAYS	1	2	3	4	5	6	7	8	9	10	11	12	13	14	15	16	17	18	19	20	21	22	23	24	25	26	27	28	29	30	31
MORNING ROUTINE																															
My Empowering Question																															
DURING THE DAY																															
My Empowering Question																															
EVENING ROUTINE																															
My Empowering Question																															
SCORE																															

Yourlife Lives™

www.yourlifelive.co.nz

It might at first glance just look like a checklist, but hey, there's nothing wrong with checklists! I do a lot of flying, mainly between New Zealand, Portugal, the UK and America, and I'm glad to know that the pilots always go through a checklist before we get into the air. A friend who's been a pilot for thirty-five years still uses his checklist every single time without fail. Pilots, doctors, engineers and other professionals use checklists to be absolutely certain that all necessary actions are taken to ensure success. That's exactly what you'll be doing when you use the Action Day by Day checklist – taking several small, but necessary, actions that will ensure your success.

Research has shown that when someone has done something for twenty-one days in a row, it becomes a habit.[12] It's drilled in at an unconscious level so it becomes more natural and automatic to *do* that thing than *not* to do it (like switching the bathroom light on when you know there's no electricity).

That said, I recently read *The 4-Hour Body: An uncommon guide to rapid fat loss, incredible sex and becoming superhuman* by Tim Ferriss,[13] which gives a slightly different view.

---

12 RS Sharma, *The Monk Who Sold His Ferrari: A remarkable story about living your dreams* (Element, 2012)

13 T Ferriss, *The 4-Hour Body: An uncommon guide to rapid fat-loss, incredible sex and becoming superhuman* (Vermillion, 27 January 2011)

So, should we use five days or thirty-one in our tools? Well, I think we want more than just to get you hooked into a process. We want it to become a completely automatic habit. While the first five days are critical in getting you hooked into your new behaviours, we've stuck with using thirty-one days so that those new behaviours really do become an automatic habit that you no longer even have to think about. Judging from the feedback we've received from the people attending our courses and the clients I work with personally, we've made the right decision. They are seeing great results by using the tools on a daily basis for the full thirty-one days.

The tools can be used to establish small changes, or to support you with major changes in your life. The main aim is to develop new habits which, by default, erase the old, unwanted ones.

Positive routines can energise you and increase your motivation. It really is as simple as 'monitoring = motivation = success'. A good friend of mine in New Zealand, Jeff Turner, records all the runs and walks he does; the time, the distance, his heart rate and how he felt. He showed this log to me. It's just an A4 sheet, all handwritten, and he loves it. He has a data watch that records all the information for him, but rather than uploading it to the website, he prefers to write it down himself. He *hates* having to write down the fact that he hasn't exercised on a day he had planned to. It really keeps him motivated and he's the fittest I have ever known him.

The Action Day by Day chart helps you establish a routine which, by the end of thirty-one days, will have become an ingrained habit, automatically guiding you towards your goal and, once you've achieved that goal, helping to keep you there.

When we were creating this tool, Mike and I reviewed many biographies and self-help books and attended seminars by highly successful people. Our research told us that successful people, whatever field they work in, all have certain long-term habits in common. It stands to reason that, given time, anyone adopting the same habits should be successful, too.

So, if you wanted to be fit and healthy, you wouldn't have to look too far to find lots of positive habits to choose from that other fit and healthy people have in common, such as: eating five portions of vegetables each day; drinking a litre of pure water; getting regular time outside in fresh air and natural daylight; doing five minutes of yoga stretches in the morning; getting some form of exercise at least three times per week, etc. The list to choose from is endless.

The key to creating your own successful checklist is to identify a whole range of *possible* habits that would help you towards your goal, and then to select just a few that you're actually willing to do. If you really hate the idea of doing something, the chances are that you won't stick with it. Set yourself up for success rather than failure by picking habits that appeal, that motivate you and that seem achievable.

I would suggest that, initially, you create a daily routine that has no more than four or five new actions over the course of the day. Be realistic. Establish those actions as a regular part of your routine. When you really feel they're integrated to such an extent that it seems natural to do them, you can add some more to your routine. There's no point in overloading yourself at the start, being unable to integrate all the new habits you're trying to form, and giving the whole thing up in frustration.

It's also a really good idea to ensure that over the course of every day, you include one habit from each of these four key areas: exercise, nutrition, mindset and passion.

You might think that *adding* to your already busy schedule is going to take time that you just don't have, but the benefits of those new habits will soon become self-evident, and in the long term, they'll *save* you time by making you more effective, efficient and focused throughout the day. If after a while those habits seem like a real drag and aren't benefitting you much, just change your routine until you find a set of habits that do work for you and keep you sailing steadily (or even better, rapidly) towards your goal.

Using your Action Day by Day checklist

The first ritual of the day is the most powerful, as it sets the context for the day ahead, and can influence how you respond to the events you encounter throughout the day.

For example, the first meal of the day is the most important, because if you mess up that one, it's easy to just say, 'The day's already a write-off as far as food's concerned, so I might as well eat rubbish for the rest of the day. I can try again tomorrow.' Whereas, if you start the day in the healthy way you planned, you'll feel the day has got off to a successful start; you're more likely to eat a good lunch, and feel motivated to keep to your plan. Really prioritise your morning routine. It'll help every day to set off in the right direction.

One part of your morning routine that I'd like to insist on is that you look at Your Life Compass to tune yourself in for the day, to immerse yourself for a few minutes in your primary goal, and remind yourself why it's so important to you. Mark that into the section for your morning routine. Then simply brainstorm the small actions you could add to your current routine that would help you to achieve your primary goal. Decide which four or five (or even just two or three) you're going to build into your daily routine from today, and write them into your checklist in the section you think they fit best – morning routine, during the day or evening routine.

The actions you put into your routine don't have to be big dramatic gestures. They can be as simple as drinking herbal tea every morning instead of your usual strong coffee, or just making a point of smiling welcomingly at your unruly teenager when you see them at the end of the day and giving them a hug if you think they'll let you (you might be surprised!), or doing ten minutes of meditation before bed. You might want to download the 'Relax Now' audio on the website. It's designed to allow you to relax and recharge.

〰️ Relax Now (audio)
https://tinyurl.com/neuralcoding

It takes just fourteen minutes and many of my clients just love to include it in their daily routine. Pick anything that will take you even the smallest step towards whatever goal you've set yourself.

I would really urge you to prioritise one particular step in your evening routine, too. Take a few minutes to plan the next day. Write down the key things you need or want to do. You'll waste less time the next day so you can just hit the ground running. You can also sleep easier knowing that your priorities are clear and that you already know what steps you'll be taking regarding any problems you need to deal with.

As you go through the day, tick the box against each action as it's done. One useful aspect of using the checklist like this is that it acts as a clear feedback system. After only a few days, you'll begin to see whether there's a pattern to what's happening. It's particularly useful for monitoring any parts of the routine that you're not managing to stick to.

When I was studying for my degree, I had as one of my daily actions one hour of study. However, on my chart, I kept seeing a cross against that hour of study – it just wasn't happening. Whenever you see a pattern like this, the first question you have to ask yourself is, 'Is this as important to me as I thought it was?' And if it really isn't that important to you, or this particular action just isn't one you really want to embrace, then you can catch it there and then and choose a different action to replace it with so you can continue towards your bigger goal.

With my daily hour of study, this wasn't the case at all. It really *was* important to me. I definitely wanted to get that degree, and I was finding the subject matter absolutely fascinating. Therefore, the next question has to be, 'What's stopping me from doing this?'

When I thought about it, I realised I was allowing myself to get side-tracked into writing programmes and designing training courses.

Just realising this was useful, and made me think about how I could plan more rigorously to make sure that I broke off from work and took that little bit of time out each day. I had to find a way of catching myself, putting the training courses to one side, and prioritising that one hour of study. If I hadn't had that checklist to flag up early on that something wasn't working, it would have been so easy to just let it slide for much longer without doing anything to address it.

My empowering question

You'll notice that next to each routine (morning, daytime and evening) there's space on the Action Day by Day checklist to write an empowering question. What are you meant to write here?

Well, let's say you're trying to slim down. You've lost a few pounds, then you hit a bit of a plateau. You've been struggling to stick with the healthy eating plan you've put in place, and you find yourself asking, 'Why does this always happen to me?' or, 'Why can I never stick to a diet?' What answers will you get back from questions like this? Probably something like, 'I'm useless,' or, 'Because I've got no willpower.' Where does this get you? Nowhere useful. It certainly won't make you feel resourceful and motivated. It's common to ask ourselves pointless and disempowering questions like this that simply lead us down into a spiral of negative thoughts.

People who achieve in life ask different questions when they're faced with a problem. Our brains are designed to answer our questions, so it's critical to make sure we ask questions that will move us forwards into a resourceful state.

When I was first learning about empowering questions, it was in January 2008 when I was on my Master Practitioner's course. I had started training for that big run across Portugal – the challenge that the SPEC-IFY model helped me so much with. There I was in New Zealand, in class from ten o'clock in the morning until six o'clock in the evening, with homework and revision to do every night while also trying to fit in running twice a day.

One of the joys of being on a course is mixing with fellow students, but in the little time that everyone had for socialising, I had to go running. Before coming across the Empowering Questions technique, I think I might have been saying to myself, 'Why did I get myself into this?' or, 'How am I meant to find time to do everything?' – neither of which would have been particularly helpful. Instead, my question to myself became, 'How can I enjoy this experience even more?' That question presupposes that there's already something enjoyable about the action you're trying to take, and sets your mind to looking for useful, supportive answers. I kept that question at the forefront of my mind the whole time. When I woke up at six o'clock in the morning to go running before breakfast, only to find it pouring with rain, rather than thinking, 'How did I get myself into this? I'm not going out in that weather!' I used my empowering question: How could I enjoy this even more? It allowed me to think, 'Well, as it's raining and I'm going to get soaked through anyway, why don't I go and run on the beach, right down by the surf, and enjoy the sound of the waves and the wind, with my feet in the sea – it'll be fun.' And oh my, it was.

There's room for an empowering question next to each phase of the day on your Action Day by Day chart, and depending on the activities you've planned for your day, you might want to think of a different empowering question for each part of your routine. Alternatively, you might find one particular empowering question that seems to help you no matter what the situation, and it's fine to just stick to that same empowering question all the time. The important thing is to find a question that opens your mind to positive possibilities and solutions.

The key thing is to think, 'Does this question move me towards my goal, or away from my goal?' Your empowering question should always move you towards your goal.

Here are some examples of empowering questions that might help you:

- How could I enjoy this even more?
- What else could this mean?

- What could I be even more grateful for?

- How can I provide more value?

- How could I make this even easier?

- What would make this even more exciting and motivating for me?

Empowering Questions (PDF)
https://tinyurl.com/neuralcoding

We have also put an 'Empowering Questions' PDF on the website for you to download. It has lots of empowering questions for you to choose from if you need some inspiration.

Reviewing your Action Day by Day checklist

Each morning when you get up, look at Your Life Compass, then follow your list of morning routine actions, in the same order each day.

Before long, if you tie in these new actions with already established habits, like brushing your teeth or showering, they'll quickly become a natural part of your routine. Set yourself up to succeed by making it easy for yourself. For example, if time's short in the morning, why not laminate Your Life Compass and stick it up for you to read thoroughly while you take your morning shower every day? Or use our Apple app or the alarm on your phone to set up regular alarms and alerts.

It's important not to get bogged down in a step that you don't like. Just change it. Find one that's more enjoyable, or find a way of doing it that *makes* it more enjoyable for you. Make use of your empowering questions to help you keep on track.

At the end of each day, there's a box to record your score for that day (ie, how many of the actions did you actually do?). It's not there to give you something to beat yourself up with! It will be motivating and it will also highlight patterns. Are there certain days of the week that you always seem to get everything done effortlessly? Are there others that you always have a low score on? Use the feedback from the checklist to flag up things like this. It allows you to analyse what's happening and think about how you might be able to change things to get them working better for you. The score can also help you put a bad day into perspective. At the time, it can really get you down, but one bad day in the middle of a load of good ones becomes just a blip that really doesn't matter when you can clearly see that, on the whole, you're doing really well.

One lady came to our Seize Your Life course in Europe. She was forty-five years old and a busy mum of two. She had been trying to lose weight for thirty years. Three months after the course, I received a lovely email from her, which said, 'I'd fretted for thirty years about trying to manage my weight, but since the 'Seize Your Life' course it's so much easier to stay on track. Also, be it coincidence or otherwise, the most effective tools to do it fell straight into my lap on that course! I'm well on my way to achieving my first goal of losing 10 kg and being leaner and fitter. I've already lost 6.5 kg and I feel great for it.'

When you reach the end of the sheet, it's time to have a review. Do you still need those actions on your checklist? Are some of them so automatic now that you don't need to be nudged and reminded about them? If that's the case, what new actions can you add to your routine that will propel you towards your goal even faster? It might be that you feel confident about just one or two of the actions, in which case you can just replace those ones with new actions and keep the rest the same. Don't let success make you go overboard and suddenly overload yourself with too many extra actions. Keep it simple and practical. It's amazing what big things can be achieved using small steps.

You will find the Action Day by Day template as well as an Action Day by Day sample on the website.

Action Day by Day (PDF)
https://tinyurl.com/neuralcoding

Print out fresh copies of the Action Day by Day checklist whenever you like.

You might even want to have more than one checklist at the same time, because in different circumstances, you might want to adapt what you do. When I'm in Portugal, my checklist is a little different to the one I use when I'm in New Zealand, because the climate's different, the resources and the landscapes are different. Sometimes, so are the people I'm around, so I adapt my routines to my circumstances. That way, I've got no excuse for not continuing to aim for that goal.

So, select your actions and fill in your checklist. Keep it simple, and don't try to change too much too quickly. Keep your checklist in full view so you'll be prompted to act on it every day. Even the busiest people can make it work if they're committed. Many busy people get up early to make use of that wonderfully calm and quiet time before everyone else is up and about. If you've selected your goals well, then the benefits will soon show, and make the early mornings definitely worth it!

So, there you go. You've got the tools now to really begin the changes that can transform your life, permanently. Go ahead and get started. I'm really excited about what the future could hold for you. I hope you are, too. In the next chapter, we're going to take a trip there – to the future – to make sure it turns out as planned!

Modelling in Japan after losing 13 kg (28 pounds) in weight

Amanda aims high

AMANDA Ryland finishes her last-minute packing before flying out to Japan on a two-month modelling contract.

Amanda, who is a former Halifax gala queen, landed the job earlier this year after sacrificing her favourite scones and chocolate to lose 21lb.

During her stay she hopes to see as much of the country as possible, including its Disneyworld.

"I'm really looking forward to the next two months, it will be a real eye-opener," said 19-year-old Amanda, of Moor End Road, Mount Tabor, Halifax.

While in Tokyo she will model designer clothes at fashion shows and do photographic and commercial work.

If more work is available after the two months is up Amanda is hoping to extend her contract and gain more experience.

Amanda will also be appearing on a TV programme being broadcast today. She was interviewed as part of a BBC "Open Air" programme on her agency, the Manchester Model Agency.

She will miss the programme but her parents, Yvonne and David, will record it for her to watch when she returns after Christmas.

They have both supported Amanda's bid to make a career of modelling and hope the Tokyo trip will be a success.

The local newspaper report about my weight loss and selection for the big contract in Japan

Doing my first triathlon while on my way to getting fit and losing all that weight again. . . sensibly this time!

My first marathon, in 2005

*Being interviewed by RTP at the end of
my run right across Portugal in 2008*

SEVEN

Creating The Future

You might think you're pretty well set up now, and you'd be right. You've worked out what your primary goal is. You're focused on it, and you know what other areas of your life you have to keep in balance while you're achieving that goal. You've worked with your unconscious mind, using the SPECIFY and SCORE tools to ensure it's on board with your plans, and you've got Your Life Compass and Action Day by Day to help you build new, positive habits and routines. You're ready to use them to keep you focused and motivated while you power your way towards that goal. You may even have already started taking action to begin your progress towards the life you want to lead.

You're already ahead of the game. You're all set up to get going. I'm not about to hold you back, but we're not leaving it there. We're going to do even more to ensure you get the life you want.

Over the next few chapters, we're going to lock your goal firmly in place, and we'll be looking at some tools and techniques that you can pull out of the bag if the going gets tough and you need a little extra help. Or, you might want to use them to get your motivation sky high, and get yourself racing sure-footedly, full speed ahead.

It's at about this stage, when you start to realise that this really could work, that you might find yourself hitting a wobbly patch. Now is when the 'what ifs' creep up on you. 'What if I don't do it?', 'What if I can't. . .', 'What if I do what I always do, and run out of steam after a couple of days?' The negative self-talk can sneak in, eroding your confidence in spite of all the good work you've been doing.

There are two clear answers you can give yourself, particularly if past failures are in danger of convincing you that you're bound to fail again. Firstly, it's really important to realise that while those past failures did happen, the 'you' back then was a different person to the 'you' now – even if back then was just last week! You didn't have the tools in place to support you and you hadn't done the unconscious work that you've done now. Even without all that, there is no reason whatsoever that you should make the same kind of choices and decisions that you made in the past. Just decide you're going to make positive, constructive choices with your goal in mind. There's no plan B, because that suggests plan A might not work, and detracts from your focus and belief in it. This is a new future you're moving towards. Embrace it. Do you remember those personality traits you're developing? Think of those role models. What would they say to your 'what ifs'?

Secondly, we're going to leave no room for, 'What if I don't manage it?', because we're about to lock the achieving of your goal into your future. Once that's done, you can always 'remember' that you've already achieved the goal. You're just in the process of catching up with it!

This may sound a little bizarre, but allowing your unconscious to create your future is really no different to what lots of people automatically do all the time. The only problem is they're usually creating the very future they *don't* want. They frequently run movies or stories in their mind of the future going wrong, even in the smallest and simplest of ways. For example, a golfer will say to themselves, 'Don't go in that bunker. Keep out of the bunker!' only to find that the very thing they were trying to avoid has just happened. It's not magic or coincidence – it's their unconscious mind at work, making small automatic movements of their body tie in with their negative thoughts.

Does that sound crazy? Well, think of it this way. Think of something that happened last week. Something simple; nothing traumatic. Bring that event to mind, close your eyes and point to where last week was for you. Good. Now open your eyes and see where your brain naturally stores your past.

Now think of a similarly simple event that's OK to think about that's going to happen next week. It doesn't have to be anything spectacular or exciting (lucky you, if it is!). Imagine it in full colour. See all you will see; hear what you'll hear and get a sense of how you'll feel – actually develop that physical feeling in your body now.

Good. Now close your eyes and point to this event. Open your eyes and see that this is how your brain stores your images of the future. You've just created a future memory. Even though this event hasn't happened yet, your brain stores this just the same as it stores a past memory.

So, let's get down to the business of creating a positive future memory and locking it into place. It's another way of making sure that your brain knows clearly what outcome you're working towards, and uses the immense power of your unconscious mind to ensure you get there.

We're going to use a timeline to do this. Time Line Therapy® was developed by Tad James[14] and it's been used in many different ways to allow people to make

14   A James, 'Time Line Therapy® training' (Tad James Co, 2023), www. nlpcoaching.com/time-line-therapy/, accessed 12 June 2023

changes. It's a serious science that falls under the umbrella of Neural Coding and it's known to work effectively. I use it a lot with my own clients, and use it all the time for myself. It's another way to ensure all your resources are working in harmony, and to make it *even more likely* that you'll achieve your goals.

When I was doing my Master Practitioner course in Auckland, a fellow student asked me if I'd covered setting a goal in the future timeline yet. I hadn't done it, and was keen to learn about it. She said she'd had some Neural Coding coaching that had included this technique, and it was this that had made her decide to train in Neural Coding herself, as she was so impressed with the outcome.

She had been preparing for her black belt in karate and one of the things she was really concerned about was the part of the grading where she would have to break a board with her foot. Every time she'd tried it in practice, she hadn't been able to get a clean strike, hadn't broken the board and had hurt her foot quite badly. The more often this happened, the more she would worry about the board not breaking and just not being able to do it. She was running this movie in her mind again and again. Of course, without realising it she was telling her unconscious mind that this is what she wanted to happen! Her unconscious mind was getting stuck on the movie she was playing over and over again in her mind, and kept reproducing the same problem. She ended up absolutely dreading doing the grading.

A short time before the grading was due to take place, she went for a Neural Coding session to try to combat the anxiety she was feeling about it. Among other things, she ended up doing some Time Line Therapy, and seeing the grading going really well in her mind, hearing her foot breaking the board with ease and feeling great afterwards. She was quite stunned to find that everything she put into the future timeline happened just as she had visualised it, and she passed with flying colours.

I was really excited to learn about this new Neural Coding tool, and I could see how it could be particularly useful for sports people who were especially anxious and nervous about a specific event that was coming up.

A short time later, I found myself working with a lady in Queenstown who was dealing with a similar situation, but in this case, it was a judo black belt that she was preparing for. Her worry was that she kept finding herself going into a kind of spasm where she would freeze, her mind would go blank, and she just couldn't think of the next thing she was meant to do. I was delighted, because I knew that this was a perfect situation to try my newly acquired Time Line skills!

We used the 'future timeline' to allow her to create a movie of what she *did* want to happen. We were sensory specific about what she would see, what she would hear and what she would feel to know that she had done a successful grading. We locked that movie into her future timeline. I received an email from her shortly after her grading took place, letting me know that everything had gone exactly to plan. Not only that, she had expected to feel nervous at the grading, instead of which, she'd felt excited in a way that made her feel really focused on the task at hand. In the end, she did much better than she'd dared to hope.

The great thing is that this is one of those tools that you can use again and again, whenever you need or want to make use of it.

Follow the exercise below, or if you prefer to let me lead you through the process personally, go to the website and watch the 'Putting your goal in your future' video.

Putting Your Goal in Your Future (video)
https://tinyurl.com/neuralcoding

Many people tend to find that easier, especially the first time they use this technique.

Have your primary goal much in mind before you begin this exercise. Look at Your Life Compass to remind yourself of the details and your motivation. Remind yourself of the positive way in which your goal is described and recall the Sensory Specific information you fed to your unconscious mind when you worked through the SPECIFY model. Try to just relax. Your unconscious mind already knows how to do this – we're just helping your conscious mind to communicate clearly and specifically about where the unconscious mind should aim for.

EXERCISE: Locking your goal in your future

Bring into your mind a picture of what it will be like when you achieve this goal that you've set yourself. You've already worked on this before, so the picture should come to mind easily. As you look at this picture of yourself having succeeded, think about what things you've done to get there; what actions you took to achieve your goal.

And now, make it more powerful by stepping right into that picture so that you can look through your own eyes. . . You can really become that person. . . the one who has just achieved your goal. . . Notice in detail. What can you see that lets you know that you've achieved that goal? What can you hear? What feelings do you have, both emotional and physical? Where in your body can you feel them? Really allow yourself to feel this. . . the absolute knowledge, without a doubt, that you've achieved what you set out to achieve. Enjoy the feeling for a few moments. Great.

Now, if we make that picture brighter, does that make the feeling more intense? If it does, keep it like that. If it doesn't, then adjust the brightness until it's just right for you. What if we make it sharper and more crisply focused? How's that? Keep it at the right focus for you. What about if we make it bigger? How does that feel? Set the picture exactly the way it needs to be for it to be at its most powerful for you. Excellent.

Now, step back out of that picture and hold it up in front of you. It might be a still picture, or it might seem like you're watching a movie of yourself. Either way, take a deep breath in, then breathe out heavily and as you breathe out imagine you're breathing vibrancy and life and colour into that image you're holding in front of you. See it growing larger, beginning to radiate with energy, becoming even more lifelike than it already was. Notice how bright and strong the colours are becoming. Notice how the volume of any sounds, any voices, increases. Notice, particularly, as you breathe life into the image, how you can feel those emotions of success more and more clearly.

Repeat the deep breath three times, each time breathing more and more vibrancy and life and feeling into that picture of you succeeding in your goal until this picture is now vibrating and glimmering and resonating with life and joy.

Now, take a firm hold of that picture and bring it with you as you allow yourself to drift up to float above your timeline. Float above yourself, above 'now'. If you look down, you'll see yourself sitting there, below you. When you're ready, float gently forwards in time, until you feel that you're over the point in time that this goal is going to be achieved. You might just get an automatic feeling about the right place (or time) to stop, or it might be indicated in some way – maybe a light shining at a particular point to guide you, a sound or maybe even a gut feeling.

When you're ready, you're going to take this picture and let it float down to be locked into your timeline. Allow the picture to float down into the timeline and hear the noise it makes as it suddenly snaps down, firmly locking into place. You can see the locks that have been triggered, holding the picture securely, fixing it at that particular time.

As you float a little higher, you see the picture, the achievement of the goal, firmly staying put, locked into your timeline for ever. Now turn from where you're floating above this future event, and look back towards 'now'. Notice how, like the ripple from a pebble dropped in water, achieving that goal has an impact. . . Notice the changes happening within the timeline on the way back to 'now' – changes that will make the goal come into being.

Whenever you're ready, float back to 'now', knowing that those events and decisions will be changed to align with the achievement of that goal now firmly fixed in your future. Once you arrive above 'now', just float there for a few minutes, noticing the feeling inside your body now that you know you've fixed in place the events that will lead to your goal being achieved. Know that your unconscious mind has been put into action, firmly targeted towards your aims. Know that it will be working towards your goals even while you're asleep. Even while you're reading or hearing this, you've given your unconscious mind whatever it needs to be able to work diligently towards your goal.

When you're ready, float back down gently into the room. . . back into your body. Take your time. Wriggle your fingers and toes, have a stretch, and bring with you that sense of purpose and the certainty that your goal is just waiting for you, that you've already achieved it in your mind and that it won't be long before your body catches up!

Remember, you can do this at any time and for any goal. It's extremely powerful, so now you can look forward to celebrating your achievements!

EIGHT

Getting Into The Zone – No Matter What!

No matter how well you're doing now, there are still going to be times when you don't feel quite as calm, focused, motivated and determined to succeed as you would like. Wouldn't it be great to be able to just press a button and immediately feel the way you need to feel? To be able to just switch on a resourceful state that would help you tackle whatever's ahead?

Well, that's exactly what a Neural Coding technique called anchoring will allow you to do. What's so great about it is that it's something you already do, quite naturally and automatically, without realising it. It's programmed into us as a kind of defence mechanism, and like all automatic functions, it's rooted at an unconscious level. It's just a case of guiding that amazing unconscious mind of ours in a direction that will support us in achieving our goals.

So, what's this new tool? Imagine you've got the radio playing in the background, and suddenly on comes a song that was around when you were much younger. It makes you smile because it brings back fond memories – perhaps a school disco, a particular boyfriend or girlfriend, or a special holiday. Hearing the music transports you straight back to that time. You see images in your mind of what was happening, and you actually feel the emotions that you felt at the time wash over you. Those particular memories and feelings have been 'anchored' to that song, and are recalled quite vividly whenever you hear it. You didn't do anything to anchor those memories to the song, it just happened automatically. Another example: maybe you walk past an open window and smell an apple pie baking in the oven. The smell sparks off in your neurology and immediately brings up memories of Grandma, who used to make fantastic apple pies. You feel a nice warm feeling inside, even though you've not eaten anything and Grandma is nowhere in sight!

Negative emotions and memories can be anchored, too. It's a perfectly normal part of learning what's safe and what's not, what's good for you and what should be avoided. For example, you might bump your car against a pillar when you're pulling out of a particular car park. It doesn't need to be anything major or traumatic, just a bit of a scrape. However, from that day on, whenever you're pulling out past that pillar, you're likely to tense up because you've anchored the unpleasant memory and feelings to that location.

Basically, we're 'anchoring machines'. There's nothing we can do about it. What we normally do is allow it to happen automatically, whether or not the emotions are suitable and useful for us. This unconscious, automatic process is often referred to as conditioning. What we're going to do is *consciously* condition a special gesture to bring about an automatic, *desirable* response that you have chosen. That's really what anchoring is all about.

The concept was developed at the beginning of the twentieth century by a professor of psychology at the University of Pennsylvania, Edwin B Twitmyer. He was studying the patellar tendon reflex (you know the one, where the doctor taps you just below the knee-cap, and your lower leg jerks). Twitmyer had created a mechanical apparatus to deliver the tap automatically against the knee. A bell was sounded to warn his subjects that the hammer was about to tap against them. On one occasion, however, the bell sounded by accident, and he noticed that the patient's lower legs jerked as normal, even though they hadn't actually been tapped at all. Twitmyer was fascinated by this, and went on to explore it in more detail and with more subjects. He found that, if the bell and hammer were used together often enough beforehand, then *all* of his subjects would respond to the bell with the reflex action, whether or not the hammer tapped them. Some of his subjects even found that they couldn't suppress the conditioned response, even if they wanted to. Twitmyer had discovered classical conditioning. However, the poor guy never got the recognition he deserved, even though he wrote a doctoral dissertation on his findings before anyone else had come up with the phenomenon.[15]

You've probably heard of the guy who *did* get all the glory: Ivan Pavlov. Three years after Twitmyer published his paper, Pavlov presented *his* findings on conditioning in dogs.[16] He had really been studying the digestive systems of mammals. It was clear that when dogs were presented with food, they began to salivate in preparation of digesting the food. However, he noticed that the dogs sometimes began to salivate when there was no food present. He soon worked out that the dogs were associating white lab coats with the delivery of food. The assistants who were carrying out the experiments always wore white lab coats when they fed the dogs, so the dogs began to react just to the presence of people in white lab coats, whether they had food or not. He explored this phenomenon using a variety of stimuli, the most commonly

15 DJ Coon, 'Eponymy, obscurity, Twitmyer, and Pavlov', *Journal of the History of Behavioral Sciences*, Jul (1982), 18(3) 255–262, https://pubmed.ncbi.nlm.nih.gov/6749963/#:~:text=Edwin%20B.,had%20little%20impact%20on%20psychology, accessed 12 June 2023

16 Wikipedia, 'Ivan Pavlov' (2023), https://en.wikipedia.org/wiki/Ivan_Pavlov, accessed 12 June 2023

quoted being a bell. For example, just before the dogs were given food, a tuning fork (or bell or whichever sound they were being conditioned to) was sounded. Before long, the dogs began to associate the tuning fork with the food and would begin to salivate just on hearing it. They had anchored receiving food to the sound of the tuning fork, and all their automatic functions responded.

To demonstrate just how automatic and fundamental this ability to anchor is, there's a much later experiment I'd like to mention. It was carried out on planaria, a kind of flatworm, in the 1960s. Now these are not the most highly evolved and intelligent of creatures – but even they can anchor efficiently! The unfortunate planaria were given a mild electric shock every time a light was flashed. The shock was enough to make them jump and recoil. After a while, if the researchers just flashed a light, the planaria still recoiled and jumped *as though* they were receiving an electric shock.[17]

So, this idea of conditioning has been widely researched, and is clearly something fundamental that we do inherently. But how do we make use of it deliberately, to anchor any emotion or state we choose, and recall it whenever we need it?

---

17 N Deochand, MS Costello and ME Deochand 'Behavioral research with planaria', *Perspectives on Behavior Science*, 9 Nov (2019), 41(2) 447–464, www.ncbi.nlm.nih.gov/pmc/articles/PMC6701699/, accessed 12 June 2023

We use a particular, deliberate gesture to be able to access these emotions or states of mind, no matter where we are. Sportsmen and women make use of this a great deal. You might have watched Jonny Wilkinson, the English rugby player. He had an amazing record for consistently scoring drop goals and penalty kicks. He had a trademark ritual he went through in preparation for taking a kick. He put his hands together in front of him and did a funny, almost squatting shuffle, took a deep breath, focused and then kicked. Almost every time, the ball went exactly where he wanted it to: between the posts. He would go through exactly the same routine every single time. This was his anchor. By doing it, he was reminding his unconscious mind of exactly what he wanted. As a result, he's one of a few players who has achieved the same level of consistency on the pitch, under pressure, as they have in practice.

Different sports people have different anchors. They find ones that work for them, and then use those anchors consistently to help them achieve excellent results. Maybe a tennis player has to bounce the ball on the base line a certain number of times before serving, or an athlete goes through exactly the same stretches and manoeuvres before settling on the blocks ready to run.

When I work with a client on anchoring, we need to decide on a simple, unobtrusive gesture. The one most commonly used is just touching the tip of the thumb and ring finger of the left hand together. It needs to be a gesture that's not likely to happen by accident. If somebody touches or fiddles with their earlobe a lot, it wouldn't be a good idea to use that action as an anchor; they would be constantly setting off the anchor without meaning to, and it would soon become completely ineffective.

What exactly do we anchor to this gesture of touching the thumb and ring finger together? Normally it's a state of mind – for example, confidence, determination, motivation, love, relaxation or peace. I work with a number of pilots in New Zealand who fly Malaysia Airline planes. Several of them have holiday homes nearby, where they will bring their families on holiday. Because many of them are constantly flying long haul, their body clocks are all over the place. Consequently, they come for a nice relaxing, peaceful holiday only to find they can't sleep!

What I do with them is set a relaxation anchor. I get them to relax a little, then to imagine an image of what real relaxation means to them. What would they be saying to themselves if they were totally relaxed? What would they see and hear that would let them know that they are relaxed? I get them to really feel that sense of relaxation. When they're really picturing that relaxed state clearly, I ask them to make the gesture: to press the tips of their thumb and ring finger together. By repeating this a few times, it anchors the state of relaxation to the gesture, so they can call up the feeling they want, whenever they want, just by pressing those fingers together.

Anchoring can be used in all sorts of situations. There's an event in New Zealand called 'Coast to Coast'. You may have heard of it. It's enormous – 243 km to be covered in one day. A guy called Steve Gurney became a bit of a legend by winning it nine times. Even as a veteran, with all the young bucks competing against him, he was still able to complete the gruelling combination of cycling, running and kayaking faster than any of them. How did he do that? Well, among other things, he set himself a lot of anchors. Some of the anchors used his hands, but a large chunk of the race involved kayaking on white water, which meant his hands were constantly busy. How did he get round that? He used his teeth! He would put his tongue through particular gaps in his teeth and that would fire off whatever anchor he needed to access, including absolute determination and confidence that he could win – again!

Steve was so impressed by the effectiveness of the anchors, and by Neural Coding in general, that he decided to train in Neural Coding himself. In fact, he's now become an instructor of Neural Coding and we sometimes run workshops together in New Zealand.

So, anchoring is really powerful stuff, and we do it naturally. It's not some kind of complicated technique that you have to train yourself to be able to do. Everyone (even a flatworm) already knows instinctively how to do it. You just have to start using it *consciously*.

When I was doing the run across Portugal, it really was a long way! One of the things I did to help me complete the run was to make sure I had programmed anchors on my fingers. I programmed one for endurance, and one for power. If I was running up a hill and it seemed to be going on forever and I started thinking, 'Help! I've got to reach the top soon. I really don't need this!' I would fire off the anchor on my right hand, the one for power, and my body would flood with the speed and strength to get me up that hill. Or, when it was getting later in the day, my mind might begin to wander off into, 'Am I actually going to make it? Can I really keep going?' and then I would fire off the anchor on my left hand, the one for endurance.

Anchoring

Now it's your turn to set some anchors. Before we begin, take a few minutes to think back through your memories. You're looking for a time when you were totally calm and relaxed. Once you've identified a time when you were calm and relaxed, move on to find a memory when you were totally motivated, firing on all cylinders. Then think of an occasion when you felt totally loved. Finally, think of a time when you were absolutely, confidently determined. With each memory, try to recall what you saw, heard and felt that helped you to know that you were totally relaxed, motivated, loved and confidently determined.

If you really can't think of a time when you experienced these states, that's OK. Simply imagine what it would be like to feel like that. You might find it useful to think about a character or situation in a movie or a book that epitomises the state you're looking for, and step into that part so that you'll be able to picture clearly, with all your senses, what it would be like.

When you're doing this exercise, it is certainly easier and more effective to sit back and listen to the audio on the website. There's a short introduction to the anchoring process, then a separate audio that takes you through the process, as if I were there with you. It makes it much more effective, as anchoring while reading can be a little tricky.

ılı·ılı· **The Anchoring Process (audio)**
https://tinyurl.com/neuralcoding

If you prefer to read it, you can follow the process by doing the exercise below.

EXERCISE: The anchoring process

First ensure you have enough space to stand up and move around a little. Stretch, easing your shoulders and neck. Let your arms hang comfortably at your sides and gaze softly at a spot on the floor about a metre in front of you. Take a deep breath, and as you breathe out, feel yourself begin to relax.

Imagine a circle, big enough for you to stand in, on the floor in front of you. You're about to use that circle to help create your personal power button. This is a term I use when we set four powerful states on the same anchor. Using this 'button' will then flood your body and mind with these four resourceful states.

It's important to practise the gesture you'll be using to anchor your positive emotions. Before you begin, take the ring finger on your left hand and press the tip of it against the tip of the thumb on the same hand. Apply quite a lot of pressure, so it's definitely not something you could do without thinking, then release. Press them together firmly again, and release. Finally, close your eyes and press them together again, increasing the pressure, and then release. Now you know what that feels like, and that you can easily do it with your eyes closed.

In a few minutes, you will need to recall those empowering memories we spoke about. When you bring those memories to mind, you'll remember them so vividly that you'll see what you saw back then. You'll be transporting yourself right back into your body, so you'll be able to hear what you heard and really feel what you felt back at that moment. As you feel that positive, emotional state begin to increase, step into that imaginary circle on the floor in front of you and press your ring finger and thumb together firmly. When you're inside the circle, you'll notice that after a moment, those emotions will begin to fade a little. The moment that happens, release your finger and thumb and step back out of the circle. This way, the anchoring gesture is only in use while you're actively and intensely experiencing the state of mind that you want to access.

You're going to repeat this process four times, and each time, you'll become much more familiar with it, and it will become more and more powerful for you.

Let's begin. Close your eyes and remember a time when you felt totally relaxed, totally calm, just at peace with the world. Maybe you were on a beach listening to the waves and feeling the sun on your skin; or perhaps you were lying under a tree reading a good book. Find a memory that works for you; a time when you just felt completely relaxed and at ease. As you allow that memory of relaxation to come to you, put yourself right back there. Step into that image and look through your own eyes. See what you saw, hear what you heard and really feel what you felt. As you start to feel that sense of relaxation flooding through you, step into your imaginary circle and press your ring finger and thumb together. You're creating your own power button on the tip of your thumb!

As soon as the feelings begin to dissipate, release that power button and step back outside the circle. Well done.

Now, open your eyes for a moment, stretch, take a deep breath and close your eyes again.

This time, I want you to think of a memory when you felt totally motivated. Maybe it was running a race or achieving something at work. . . a complete feeling of motivation, when your body was tingling with energy and you simply wanted to get on and do the best you possibly could. As you think about that memory and picture it, float down into that image and become yourself in it – see what you saw, hear what you heard and really feel what you felt in that motivated state.

As you allow that state to flow over you now, and you feel your body begin to tingle with motivation, step inside that circle and press your power button.

As soon as it starts to dissipate, step out and release the power button. Well done. Open your eyes and look around you. You might check what the weather's doing outside before you close your eyes again.

This time, we're looking for a memory when you felt really loved. Totally loved. As before, when you embrace the memory so completely that you begin to feel that love flooding through your body, make sure you're in that picture, looking through your own eyes, really seeing what you saw, hearing what you heard and feeling what you felt, and as that love starts building up, you know what to do.

OK, when the feeling has faded a little and you've stepped back out of the circle, open your eyes again. Look around, check what the time is, then concentrate again.

This time, I want you to recall a memory where you felt totally confident - so confident that you knew you were capable of achieving whatever you had set your mind to. Throw some determination in there as well. . . maybe somebody said you wouldn't be able to do something, and you were determined to prove them wrong. Recall that memory full of confidence and determination. Float down into that picture. Look through your own eyes - see what you saw, hear what you heard, feel what you felt. You know what to do. As you feel that determination and confidence building up, step into that circle, press the thumb and fingertip together. As the feeling dissipates, step back out of the circle.

Now, open your eyes. Bend down and pick up that imaginary circle on the floor. As you hold it in your hands, imagine squeezing and squashing it, making it smaller and smaller until it's just a small, red circle. Imagine pressing that red circle onto the end of your thumb. You've now got your power button right there, ready for you to use whenever you want or need the emotions that you've just programmed into it.

Take a short break... Stretch... Think about the things you're looking forward to doing, the ways you're aiming to change your life. Feel a sense of satisfaction and pleasure that you're actually doing something about it. Remind yourself that you can revisit any of the exercises in this book or on the website whenever you want to and that you can call on the positive states we've been visiting in this exercise just by pressing your thumb and ring finger together.

Finally, let's try out this power button. Keeping your eyes open, just stand there and press your finger and thumb together with the same amount of deliberate pressure as before. Notice what happens – notice how good it feels. The great thing is, this can be accessed without anyone else knowing. It gives you control of your emotional state any time you like.

If you happen to find yourself quite naturally experiencing a state of confidence, determination or relaxation, catch that moment and 'load up' your anchor. For example, if you've set the ring finger of the left hand as an anchor for confidence, and you find yourself in a situation where you just feel brimming with confidence, you can press the finger and thumb together to reinforce and load the anchor back up, making it even more effective. Naturally occurring states are the most powerful ones to anchor. In exercises like this one, we usually use remembered states. They can be effective, but they're made even more powerful if they're boosted with naturally occurring states.

Now, it's possible that you might want to isolate each of these powerful states. You can revisit this exercise and set up each of these states with a different anchor. Say, for example, you want to have relaxation at your fingertips as the pilots I work with do. For this, you would simply anchor relaxation on your little finger and thumb rather than your ring finger. You would do the anchoring three times on that little finger to intensify the feeling of relaxation. Whenever you wish to access that state, you would now have it at your fingertips. You can choose a different finger, or completely different anchor, for each state, while still having that super-power button programmed on your ring finger so that you can hyper-boost your state of mind and body with all four resourceful states whenever you want to.

Clients I've worked with have used this power button technique for a wide variety of purposes: public speaking, sports, dating, business, creativity, sexual intimacy – you name it. The power button's the way to go for any time a person wants to feel in control when they might otherwise be feeling negative or unhelpful emotions. You've got it there now, right at the tip of your fingers.

NINE

Hidden Saboteurs

One day, a new client came to see me in New Zealand. She was on holiday visiting some friends, and at dinner one evening they had got talking about the fact that she wasn't feeling great about her life. As it happened, the woman she was visiting was a client of mine, and she suggested that I might be able to help her.

So, I found myself sitting down to do a consultation with a beautiful, slim, articulate and intelligent twenty-eight-year-old woman. She had been through medical school, achieving the highest possible grades in all her exams, graduating with flying colours and landing an excellent job as a doctor on a ward in a major Australian hospital. She was successful and attractive, yet she was sitting there telling me that she was completely *unsuccessful* when it came to relationships.

As we talked about how this problem manifested in her life, it soon became clear that there was a lot more to it than just struggling with intimate relationships. She didn't like to play games like Trivial Pursuit, quizzes, crosswords or anything else that would challenge her intelligence. She would make up any excuse to avoid doing these activities with her family, and it all seemed to be based on a fear that she might be revealed as not being as intelligent as everyone thought she was. In spite of all the evidence to the contrary, she believed, deep down, that she was stupid.

She *thought* that she was coming to see me about the fact that she would keep people at arm's length, and push them away when she got into a relationship. However, as we explored it more, it became clear that this was just one of many symptoms. They all pointed towards the fact that, despite how well she had done, she didn't believe she was bright, so how could she possibly be a good doctor? She felt all the time that, one day, she would make a massive blunder with a dreadful misdiagnosis. Then the whole world would see her for what she really was – a stupid failure, a fraud who had the cheek to think she was capable of being a doctor.

Why am I telling you this story? Because it illustrates the fact that sometimes, even when we're motivated and successful, and seem to be doing all the right things, there's a deeply buried negative belief that nags away at us, tripping us up and preventing us from being able to truly enjoy our successes. We're often totally unaware of this thorn in our side. This beautiful, brilliant woman hadn't a clue, until our consultation, that she fundamentally believed that she was stupid and constantly afraid of people finding out.

When we worked on this limiting belief, she realised it had been installed when she was young and had been repeatedly told by one particular teacher that she was stupid. This was compounded by the fact that her mum, not meaning anything by it, would frequently say in a joking manner, 'Oh, don't be so stupid. . .' Her unconscious mind had taken on board these comments from two important and influential adults in her life and assumed they were true. The unconscious mind isn't there to question our beliefs; it simply supports them to the best of its ability.

The doctor didn't *consciously* believe that she was stupid. If she had, she would never have even considered going to medical school and training as a doctor. She knew that she was bright, so she applied herself and did well. However, this didn't make any difference to the fact that, *unconsciously*, she still *knew* that she was stupid.

So, we made some changes to that belief system. At a conscious *and* unconscious level, we changed, 'I'm stupid,' to, 'I'm capable of doing whatever I put my mind to.'

The changes in her life have been dramatic. She's discovered that she really *is* capable of doing whatever she puts her mind to. She now has the conviction and belief that she *is* a good doctor, that she *is* an intelligent human being. If she really doesn't want to play Trivial Pursuit she doesn't have to, but she now knows that she *can* play and make a good fist of it and have fun, because she doesn't have anything to prove or to hide. More importantly, she feels free to be who she is. She no longer worries about people finding out that she's a fraud, because she knows that she's just being herself. As a result, she no longer needs to keep potential partners at arm's length. She knows there's nothing to hide.

I found it easy to empathise with this client. I knew first-hand what limiting beliefs can do. When I was a little girl, it was my dream to be a vet when I grew up. I was enthralled at the thought of taking all sorts of sick and injured animals and making them well again. I couldn't imagine anything more exciting and fulfilling. At the age of seven, my life's purpose seemed crystal clear.

Then the deputy head mistress of the school told me that I couldn't possibly be a vet. Only the cleverest, most academic pupils could get into veterinary school and only the best and brightest of those would actually qualify. She made it quite clear that I was definitely not going to be one of them. I believed her. After all, she was an adult and in a position of authority, so if she thought I was too stupid to be a vet, it must be true. For the rest of my school career, I focused on sports and art. I fulfilled my belief that I was stupid by having to sit my Maths O Level three times and failing my English Literature A level, putting paid to my plans to go to college to study P.E. and English and become a teacher.

Limiting beliefs like these can be easily installed into a young person's psyche. Their conscious mind isn't fully formed yet, and their critical faculty hasn't developed, so there's no 'gatekeeper' to repel limiting and unhelpful beliefs.

Fortunately, it worked out for me when I stumbled into my career with the Estée Lauder Corporation. I quickly flourished and rose through the ranks, and that was when I began to realise that this idea that I was rubbish at maths and wasn't bright just wasn't true. I was excelling in my field and I grasped the maths involved easily. When you're working in a corporate climate, especially in the sales side, you really have to have a strong grip on maths to know what you're doing. Of course, once I realised that actually I *was* bright, it set me free to go even further, taking my degree in clinical hypnotherapy. I'm now working on my master's degree and I plan to go on and do a doctorate after that. I no longer have any reason to think that I might not achieve these goals.

I firmly believe that the deputy head was wrong to say what she said. She *could* have said, 'If you really, passionately want something and you're prepared to put whatever time and effort is needed into it, even if it's challenging and difficult, anything's possible.' But the judgement that I wasn't clever enough literally made me think to myself, 'Oh well, I won't bother trying.' And that limiting belief ran all the way through from when I was seven until about the age of twenty-five. As Henry Ford famously said, 'Whether you believe you can do a thing or not, you are right.'[18] Getting rid of that limiting belief was one of the most liberating and empowering things I've ever done.

So, it's really important to root out and identify any limiting beliefs that may be getting in *your* way and holding you back, in spite of your best intentions and the hard work you've already done.

What can we do about limiting beliefs?

The first thing to establish is that our beliefs, whether they're limiting or empowering, aren't the truth. They're just things we think. They *feel* real to us. Other people have different beliefs, which feel real to them. None of these beliefs are objectively true.

---

18 https://quoteinvestigator.com/2015/02/03/you-can, accessed 2 June 2023

For example, if I were to ask you to tell me what you believe about yourself, and then I asked your spouse, children, parents and friends what *their* beliefs about you are, chances are there would be some overlaps and quite a few differences. Nobody is absolutely right or wrong. Different people simply believe different things.

Limiting beliefs are the things you believe about yourself that limit your abilities, and especially your ability to make the most of the opportunities that come your way. Sometimes we're aware of these negative beliefs, while at other times we're not, because they're unconscious. They may be founded or unfounded. However, limitations are actually a product of the mind. In reality there are no limitations on a person. Anything can be done if you put your mind to it.

Now hang on, you might think. There are some things that can't just be brushed aside. If I'm wheelchair bound, I'm hardly going to be able to achieve my dream of being a mountaineer, right? Wrong! If that's what you choose to believe then, of course, you're absolutely right, but South African Bern Goosen chose to believe differently. As a result, in November 2007 he reached the summit of Mount Kilimanjaro, breaking his own world record for the fastest wheelchair ascent. To formally hold the world record he had to push himself for more than 90% of the entire climb without any physical help from anyone else. It was an extraordinary achievement that most people would have considered impossible. Bern was born with cerebral palsy and is officially classed as quadriplegic, yet one of his fundamental beliefs is that life is what you make it, whatever your circumstances.

The job of the unconscious mind is to support our beliefs, whatever they might be. When a belief is installed (often by the age of five or six), the unconscious mind doesn't evaluate it. It just accepts that it's true and then goes about its job of looking for evidence to support that belief. It's exceptionally good at finding that evidence, whatever that belief happens to be. If you believe that you're hopeless at maths, you'll only notice the times when you make mistakes, misunderstand maths problems, calculate the wrong change in a shop, etc. All the times that you work things out perfectly well, and all the maths-related skills that you use successfully on a daily basis, will go completely unnoticed. This is because they don't support your belief that you're hopeless in this aspect of life. On the other hand, if you believe you're good at maths, then you can experience exactly the same things, but now you'll notice how often you get things right, understand quickly and use your maths skills successfully. The times you run into difficulties or make mistakes will just be seen as uncharacteristic slip-ups and unimportant.

Beliefs don't reflect the objective truth; they just feel like they do. In which case, if we're going to believe something, let's choose to believe something empowering.

The unconscious isn't going to question it. It'll just go out and look for evidence to prove that it's true. This might manifest in small changes in behaviour, or finding ourselves saying or doing things we never would have before, things that fall into line with being that kind of person or holding that new belief.

Fortunately, using Neural Coding we can extract our limiting beliefs and install more positive ones. That sounds simple enough, but one of the trickiest things is trying to figure out just what our limiting beliefs are. They're often so ingrained that we're just not aware of them at all, because they run unconsciously, below the radar. They may have stemmed from things people said to us or about us while we were growing up, or at key points in our lives. Spending a lot of time with negative, pessimistic people can cultivate limiting beliefs, as can immersing ourselves in TV programmes, films, books or songs that affect us negatively. Knowing this and avoiding these situations can help us avoid developing those limiting beliefs even further, but how will we find out what *hidden* beliefs are already well established and holding us back?

There's a great book called *Virus of the Mind: The revolutionary new science of the meme and how it can help you* by Richard Brodie which looks at how viruses are spread from one mind to another.[19] We're not talking about real viruses here, but rather, how a belief can

---

19   R Brodie, *Virus of the Mind: The revolutionary new science of the meme and how it can help you* (Hay House, 4 June 2009)

spread from one mind to another. These can be gene-alogical, such as 'we've always had bad hips in our family' or, 'all the women in our family suffer from depression'. The question is whether this is true or whether it becomes true due to a mind virus.

Recently I was reading another book called *Born to Run: The hidden tribe, the ultra runners, and the greatest race the world has never seen* by Christopher McDougall.[20] In it he describes how he went to Copper Canyon, Mexico, to run with the Tarahumara tribe, the ancient running people. One day, he ran up a huge 2,500 ft mountain and when he reached the top he sat down for a rest, absolutely shattered. Then he saw an old man, at least seventy-five, running up just behind him. The old man smiled and sat next to Chris, saying (through a translator), 'Beautiful view from up here. I love it.' He looked relaxed and serene.

Chris couldn't believe it. This old guy had just run up this mountain as fast as Chris had, yet he seemed in no discomfort. No one had ever told him that he should not be running up mountains at his age. No one had spread a mind virus saying, 'You'll have bad hips or knees by the time you're sixty,' so he just kept running, smiling and enjoying.

Be mindful of the negative mind viruses that come your way. Just delete them. Literally say 'Delete'

---

20   C McDougall, *Born to Run: The hidden tribe, the ultra-runners, and the greatest race the world has never seen* (Profile Books, 15 April 2010)

inside your head. Embrace the ones that work for you and ignore the ones that don't.

Zapping limiting beliefs

A session with a good coach or therapist could soon unearth the key negative beliefs you hold, but with a little focus and thought, you can usually find the major ones you need to work on for yourself.

Take some time to think about and listen to the phrases you often say to or about yourself when things don't go quite to plan. Is, 'I'm such an idiot!' one of your most frequent sayings? Or, 'Why do I always end up in a mess like this?' or, 'I'm useless!' or, 'Why can't I do anything right?'

Language patterns like these are often direct pointers to underlying beliefs that we're stupid or useless and that nothing we do is ever going to be right, or that we don't deserve to be happy. It's not true, of course, but if that belief has been ingrained for years, we've spent a long time gathering lots of evidence that we're stupid and useless! And, of course, if you fundamentally believe this of yourself, you're unlikely to follow your ambitions or do the exciting things you really want to, because what's the point? It'll only go wrong, won't it? You'll just be exposed for the useless individual you know you really are. You can see why they're called *limiting* beliefs: they stop us from doing the things we could or might want to do.

A great way of noticing this is to observe yourself for a week. Notice what you say to yourself and watch what you do. Ask yourself, 'What do I believe about myself that allows me to say this, or do this?' Notice what comes up for you.

Below are some of the most common limiting beliefs that my colleagues and I encounter in our sessions with clients and on the two-day 'Seize Your Life' courses. Do any of these have a resonance for you? Do any of them feel uncomfortably familiar?

- I'm not good enough to. . .

- I'm not worth it.

- I'm too (fat, thin, old, young, stupid, etc) to be able to. . .

- I don't deserve. . . (eg, to be loved).

- I'm not (intelligent, strong-willed, beautiful) enough to. . .

- I don't like / I hate myself.

Almost all of these limiting beliefs distil down to not being good or worthy enough in some way.

Sometimes clients come to me asking for more self-esteem or more confidence. It might seem obvious that their limiting beliefs are, 'I have no confidence,' or, 'I'm shy.' However, these are actually the *symptoms* of a deeper limiting belief. What we really need to figure out is what the client believes at a deep level that makes them lack confidence, and makes them feel shy. That core belief is what causes the lack of confidence or shyness, and because they feel that way so much of the time, they begin to believe that this is just how they are. Rather than working at the surface level, trying to build self-esteem and banish their shyness, I prefer to work with the client to find out what is at the bottom of the well. What's the core, underlying belief that creates ripples and causes these other behaviours? If we can find and change what is at the core, then a similar *positive* set of ripples occurs, changing the client's behaviour and experience of themselves.

So, when you've observed your patterns of speech and thought, and worked out which underlying beliefs seem to be most relevant to you, you may well find that one particular belief is affecting you more than any other; one that really jumps out at you when you think back over issues you've had in the past, and patterns that you continue to repeat.

Once you have an idea of what that limiting belief is, write it down and let's see if we can change this to a belief that serves you better.

What would you rather believe about yourself? Often when we're clear about exactly what the limiting belief is, it can simply be changed to its polar opposite. Therefore, 'I don't deserve to be happy' becomes, 'I deserve to be happy'. Instead of, 'I hate myself', you can quite consciously *choose* to believe, 'I love myself'. That's right, you can simply *decide* that you're going to believe something much more positive. You might know right away what it is you would rather believe about yourself, but here are a few of the new, empowering beliefs that clients and course attendees most commonly find useful:

- I can. . .

- I'm intelligent.

- I'm capable of doing whatever I put my mind to.

- I have everything I need inside me.
  I am resourceful.

- I am so much more than I already know.

- I deserve. . .

- I *am* good enough.

Your unconscious mind will always support your beliefs. It's always doing its best for you. It will go out and find the evidence to support this new belief, just as it did with the old, limiting belief. That's what's so great about the unconscious mind. It'll support you either way, so let's get it to support an empowering belief rather than a limiting one.

Let's look at an example of how the unconscious mind will go out and find new evidence within forty-eight hours of a belief change.

Working with a client based in Canada, we found that she had a limiting belief that she was in no way special. This is just another version of the common beliefs of, 'I'm not worth it' or, 'I'm not good enough'. With every client, I ask them to send me an observation email forty-eight hours after our session. This gives enough time for things to become evident to most people.

This is the list I got from my client.

Dear Amanda,

Here's how my newly installed belief has shifted things for me in the last forty-eight hours:

1) I see that when I spoke about the new company I'm building, I used to tell myself, 'It'll never happen, you're just dreaming, you don't have what it takes.' Now that I've noticed that this conversation was there, it's gone. I'm no longer having that conversation with myself.

2) I had a call today with two people with really impressive CV's. I would previously have felt insecure around them, but this time I felt comfortable about feeling 'special'. I did not turn to my usual, 'Oh gosh, you guys are so great, I wish I was half

of what you are,' dance. Yet I was not being conceited, either.

3) In a presentation I gave today to thirty managers, I felt a comfort I've never felt before. When I've presented to groups like this in the past, I see now that I was telling myself, 'You don't have anything to offer. They'll soon see that you don't have what it takes.' On top of that, I would force myself to come across as confident. This time I was just naturally confident. People saw me as special. They compared me favourably to leading speakers I aspire to.

4) I used to have to sit down to write out what was going on in my head. I needed to dump out a lot of negative thoughts to try to clear my mind. I would do this every day or two. However, yesterday and today, I found that there was just nothing like that to say.

Thank you so much, Amanda. That last session was so powerful and life-altering for me.

I'm going to say something that might seem a little odd now, and that is that I haven't included a full belief change exercise in this book. It would seem to naturally fit at this point, wouldn't it? But it's all to do with ecology. Remember that bit? It would be easy to stick something in here to do the job, and yet if I'm completely honest, it would feel wrong to me. Let me explain.

My experience of working with hundreds of clients, and removing their negative, limiting beliefs easily and effectively, has left me with a genuine conviction that this is far better done in a session with an experienced coach, who has been trained to work with core belief changes.

I'm so passionate about the power of this that I insist that all our new graduates who attend our Ultimate Transformational course are thoroughly trained to do this. We spend a day-and-a-half just concentrating on this process. Most Neural Coding schools don't bother teaching it because it takes too long, but I'm determined to avoid falling into the trap of popping a simple, 'Let's travel through time and zap that limiting belief' technique into the book.

In order for it to work, and really work quickly and easily, a coaching session is definitely the best way to go.

I'm not suggesting you can only do this with one of our Your Life Live It coaches or with me. Just check that whoever you decide to work with has experience, has used it lots of times and has had great results.

Most coaches do online sessions – in fact, about 85% of my clients work with me through ZOOM and the results are great.

And it is powerful stuff. If you've been able to relate to any of this section on limiting beliefs, and you feel, 'Yes, I need to do work here,' then make time to do just that. It takes about an hour. Really! That's all. Just one hour. Most clients can't believe that they waited so long when they realise how easy it is to change.

Go for it. Email me and I'll help you find a coach in your area who has experience in belief change work. It really is worth it.

Conclusion

With all the skills and tools, the new ways of thinking, the insights, the resources and, most importantly, the power of your unconscious mind, you now know that *you're* in the driving seat. You really do get to pick the life you want, and by using all of the things that we've made available to you through both the book and the website, that's exactly what you'll be doing.

If you want to read more about how well these tools and techniques work, take a look on the website. There's a lot of information on there to help you. You might also wish to read my number 1 best selling book *Knowing You*, which is a deep dive into the world of belief change. There, you can read heartfelt stories of change and success from our clients.

FAQs (web page)
https://yourlifeliveit.com/pages/faq

You can go back to the resources on the website time and time again, using them for different states you might want to anchor, putting new goals in your timeline, designing the habits you want to develop with Action Day by Day and keeping on track with Your Life Compass. Whenever you need clarity, use the SCORE process.

If you have a friend who needs help, feel free to introduce them to the resources on the website. I'm not bothered about whether they've bought the book. I know these tools work and I want to get them into as many hands as possible so people can take control of their lives. I also know that when people make changes, they want to share it with those they love. Of course, I'd love them to buy the book, but it's more important that they make changes in their lives. Go ahead and tell them about the website and give them the password. Help them to access the resources that you have found valuable, and to realise that they are so much more than they ever thought.

Writing this book has been a great way to fulfil my mission, which is to help others to live the life they want. I am always looking for ways to improve, so if you have any ideas or suggestions, then wing them through to me. By now you know where to go on the website. Ask me questions; connect with me; connect with our coaches; use us.

Before I sign off, I would like to share one last story with you, and ask you to do one final exercise.

Like many young girls, I was completely pony mad. I really, really wanted a pony of my own, and I had done since I was about seven years old. When I was thirteen, Dad arranged for me to work at the local riding stables which were about a mile and a half up the road. I would work from 8.00 am until 6.00 pm every Saturday and Sunday, and in return, once a fortnight I would get a free ride. My dad thought this was a great idea because he wanted me to learn properly about what was involved in looking after and owning horses. He also wanted to check just how determined I was to stick with this before he would even consider buying me my own pony. *I* thought it was great because I got to spend loads of time with all these wonderful ponies, including getting to ride them now and again.

Working at the stables just confirmed to me how much I longed for a horse of my own – the owner of the stables didn't *always* remember to give me my free riding lesson or hack, but if I had my own pony, I would be able to ride it whenever I wanted.

So, I sat down and imagined what it would be like when I had my own pony. I had such a clear image of how life would be that I actually wrote a letter to myself, describing it.

On the envelope, I wrote, 'To Amanda and her Pony'. Then I got a sheet of Thelwell writing paper, and started writing.

> Dear Amanda,
>
> By the time I am reading this letter I will have my own pony. He's very fat and very fun and I love going to pony club camp with him. He loves doing clear rounds and is quite naughty and cheeky but all the other ponies love him. I win lots of rosettes with him and I'm really, really happy. In fact, I'm the happiest I've ever been in my entire life!
>
> I love Mum and Dad for buying me my pony. He nips my bottom when I'm tightening his girth, and sometimes he stands on my toes while he's eating his food. So, thank you so much Mum & Dad for buying me my pony. I really, really love him.
>
> From Amanda (without her Pony)

I sealed the envelope and planned to open it when I got my pony. In fact, my dad bought me my pony a couple of months later. He was a tubby chestnut Connemara. He was lots of fun and nipped my bottom and stood on my feet just as I'd imagined. In retrospect, it was quite amazing how closely reality mirrored the image I had created for myself.

I completely forgot about the letter, until I was twenty-six and just getting married. I was going through some of my old things that had been boxed up and stored in the attic of my parents' house, when I came across the still-sealed envelope. I opened it and read it in amusement. I was pretty impressed at how focused I had been on exactly what it would be like when I had achieved that goal of owning my own horse.

This idea of writing a letter to your future self is something that Tony Robbins uses in his conferences, and Mike and I use it in our 'Seize Your Life' courses, too. It's what I'd like you to do now, as the final exercise in the book.

Letter to Self (PDF)
https://tinyurl.com/neuralcoding

EXERCISE: Letter to self

Think about a time in the future, when you've achieved your main goal. Picture that future self, and think about what your life will be like by then.

You're going to write a letter to yourself, as though you've already achieved what you want. Think about the following questions when you write it:

- Who are you deciding to be?

- What is important to you?

- What new beliefs do you have?

- Who do you want to surround yourself with?

- What do you want to add to the world?

- What would you like to remind yourself about?

Write the letter in the present tense: 'I am. . .', 'I believe. . .', 'I am surrounded by. . .'

When you've written your letter, seal it in an envelope, write your address on it and stick on a stamp. Give your letter to a really good friend or family member – somebody who you know is going to be in your life for a long time to come. Write a date on the back of the envelope to indicate when you want the friend to post it to you. Make sure the date is at least six months ahead.

Ask your friend to make a note or set a reminder for themselves to make sure they post it when the time comes.

By the time the letter is posted, you'll have forgotten about it, so it will come as a lovely surprise when it lands on your doormat after six months, a year, two years or whatever timescale you've set yourself. It will let you see just how much you've achieved. It will remind you of what is really important to you. Send it with confidence and love and respect for your future self, knowing that you'll make it.

And now it's time for me to leave you to get on with that amazing, wonderful future that you're already starting to create.

I have recorded a message for you. It's a thirty-minute hypnosis audio that I'd like you to listen to three times a week for the first month, then once a week for the next three months. It's called 'Final message to your unconscious mind process', and it is a wonderful way to relax while allowing your unconscious to absorb the messages you want it to take on board, continually reminding yourself about what it is you want.

Final Message to Your Unconscious Mind Process (audio)
https://tinyurl.com/neuralcoding

Remember to share the website and password with anyone you think could benefit from it.

Your last audio is called 'Final say'.

Final Say (audio)
https://tinyurl.com/neuralcoding

And finally, I want to say a big thank you for investing in you. *You're* the one that makes the changes. All I do is put the remote control into your hands and guide you. For me, it is about you taking control and not waiting until another day. There is no time like the present – and that is what it is, a present you give to yourself. Well done. You're on your way. Go well. Use all the resources you now have, and start being the designer of your life.

It's Your Life... Live It.

Acknowledgements

There are so many people to thank. I could just do the 'thanks to all' trick. However, I'm going to run the risk of leaving someone out to acknowledge people personally, so here goes. If I have forgotten you, I know you are forgiving, so thank you.

To my wife Sarah who always supports, pushes and encourages me to deliver my very best and for giving the two best gifts in my entire life, our twin boys.

To my wonderful late husband Keith, without whose patience with this project it would have taken longer to get off the ground.

To Glynn Ryland, my brother who first suggested writing a book, you seed-planter, you.

To all our Neural Coders, thanks for giving back, contributing and knowing your stuff. To all our graduates, for your passion to learn life-changing stuff. To my clients, without whom I would not have learned all I have. You truly are geniuses. To my fellow Neural Coding comrades, for your support and feedback. To my teachers and mentors, Richard, Julia, Tad, Adriana, Morris, Joseph, Joan, Jennifer, Michelle and, of course, Milton, Virginia, Robert, Steven, Richard and John. Andy Austin, for his generous online calls and Nick Kemp for bringing Frank's work to us. And to Lynn, you know who you are.

And to my family and friends. To Mum and Dad, what great parents you are. For the insightful learnings that made me who I am today, thank you. To my sister blister, love you to the moon and back. To all my wonderful friends. I am lucky enough to run out of fingers when counting you. And Bud. . . Where would I be without you?

And finally, to Gilly Willian, who threw that NLP book at me all those years ago at the poolside in Portugal and said, 'Hey Amanda, have a read of this. I think you might like it.'

And so, the adventure continues…

The Author

 Dr Amanda Foo-Ryland is a mother and wife, best-selling author and the founder of Your Life Live It. She lives in Portugal and spends some time in New Zealand, with her wife Sarah and twin boys Jasper and Noah. She is the author of two books, a TEDx and Amazon Prime Speak UP speaker, and writes for various columns and publications. Her previous book *Knowing You* was also published by Rethink Press. She is passionate about change work and letting people know that change can be both fast and long lasting.

Your Life Live It was founded in 2008 and has many Neural Coders who are part of the company, working with thousands of clients around the globe daily. Amanda trains people in Neural Coding.

In her spare time, Amanda loves to run.

You can connect with Amanda:

✉ amanda@yourlifeliveit.com

🌐 www.yourlifeliveit.com

For more about Amanda and group belief change work within business:

🌐 https://creatingdreamteams.com

f https://m.facebook.com/yourlifeliveit

in http://linkedin.com/in/amandafoo-ryland

Amanda's TEDx Talk: https://youtu.be/L4UTIsnY3-Q